Govern Differently

GOVERN DIFFERENTLY

AN ACADEMICS-FOCUSED GOVERNANCE MODEL
AND HOW TO USE IT FOR GOOD

Aaron Salt

Senexus Press

Published by Senexus Press, LLC.
Colorado Springs, CO
senexuspress.com

Copyright © 2026 Aaron Salt.

All rights reserved. No portion of this book may be reproduced, stored in a retrieval system, or transmitted in any form or by any means—electronic, mechanical, photocopy, recording, scanning, or other—except for brief quotations in printed reviews or articles, without the prior written permission of the copyright owner and the publisher of this book. For permission requests, contact: info@senexuspress.com.

The scanning, uploading, and distribution of this book via the Internet or via any other means without the permission of the publisher is illegal and punishable by law. Please purchase only authorized electronic editions and do not participate in or encourage electronic piracy of copyrighted materials. Your support of the author's work is appreciated.

All web links in this book were verified as active and accurate at the time of publication. The author and publisher are not responsible for websites or their content that may have changed, moved, or become inactive since publication. If you discover a broken or changed link, please contact aaron@chalkforge.com with "Link Update" in the subject line.

This book reflects the author's personal experiences and opinions regarding school board governance. Examples and anecdotes are drawn from the author's service on public education boards and involve matters of public record. Some identifying details have been modified to protect the identity of those involved. The views expressed are those of the author and do not necessarily represent the views of any organization with which the author has been affiliated.

The information provided is for educational purposes and should not be construed as legal advice. School boards should consult with qualified legal counsel regarding specific matters and compliance with applicable laws and regulations.

ChalkForge™ and the ChalkForge logo are trademarks of ChalkForge, LLC. All other trademarks mentioned in this book are the property of their respective owners and are used for reference purposes only. No sponsorship or endorsement is claimed or implied.

Book and Cover design by TheoryTwelve, LLC.

First published in 2026.

ISBN-13: 979-8-9941135-0-9 (paperback)
ISBN-13: 979-8-9941135-1-6 (ebook)

Library of Congress Control Number: 2026902800

Proudly written, developed, and printed in the United States of America.

To Cortney and our tribe.

I hope this book accounts for all of the missed dinners, bedtimes, and sporting events during my time on the board. I appreciate all the support over the past decade. You are my world. I love you all.

Table of Contents

Introduction	1
Values-Based Governance In Practice	9
Part I: The Foundation	17
Chapter 1: Introduction to VBG	19
Chapter 2: Framing Governance	31
Chapter 3: Defining Values	55
Chapter 4: Leadership Challenges	69
Part II: The Model	83
Chapter 5: Values-Based Governance	85
Chapter 6: Strategic Alignment	97
Chapter 7: Policy Development	105
Chapter 8: Cultural Adaptation	121
Part III: The Strategies	133
Chapter 9: First Things First	135
Chapter 10: Understanding the "A" Word	151
Chapter 11: Sustainable Change	181
Chapter 12: Other Key Strategies	193
Part IV: The Resources	205
Chapter 13: Implementation Timeline	207
Chapter 14: Assessment and Planning Tools	215
Chapter 15: New Board Member Survival Kit	225
Chapter 16: Troubleshooting Guide	231
Conclusion	241
About the Author	249
Acknowledgments	251

"A genuine leader is not a searcher for consensus, but a molder of consensus."

– *Dr. Martin Luther King, Jr.*

Introduction

I've been booed, cheered, and haggled by both Satanists and religious zealots. But, more importantly, I've been effective. Despite this book's size, it contains some big ideas that will challenge your thinking and attitude towards governance. Values-Based Governance, which I'll explain in detail in Part II, is a framework for effective governance based on my decade of experience. I'm introducing it in this book so you, too, can be an effective leader in public governance.

Values-based Governance (or VBG) isn't a complex concept to understand, but it can be difficult to internalize and implement. My goal with this book is to present the following chapters in small, bite-sized chunks that define this framework and equip you to start implementing VBG with your school board. I've also included a complete implementation roadmap with timelines and practical tools to guide your journey. These tools will make your board and your organization more effective and efficient in serving your students and community.

Local Government Makes America Great

Our founding fathers established our country on the principle of public service. From our very beginning, American citizens have stepped up to serve their communities. Service in local government is one of the things that has made this country the global leader it is today. We are a country of tiny cities and counties, spread across every state in the Union, serving as the building blocks of our beloved nation.

Unfortunately, there is a dearth of citizens willing to take on leadership roles. Society needs stronger leaders to help public institutions achieve their goals and steward resources more sustainably and responsibly. As a leader, this is an opportunity for you to pick up the torch and make a difference in your community. And we need *you* to step into the arena and make a difference.

Importance of School Boards

Most of my experience has come from sitting on public school boards. I've worked with members of educational boards from individual schools, districts (both large and small), and state-level boards. I have witnessed the impact these educational institutions can have on our students' outcomes. And let's be very clear: today's students are tomorrow's leaders. We need them to be as educated, equipped, and prepared as possible.

Serving on a school board isn't the most alluring role you can have in local government, but honestly, you would be hard-pressed to find a more rewarding and fulfilling position. One of the greatest highlights of my life was handing out diplomas to our graduates. I served in a district with seven high schools, so we spent two-and-a-half days in graduation ceremonies every year. They were long days, but celebrating these kids—some of whom are the first in their families to graduate—as they walk across the stage with big,

Introduction

goofy grins to receive their diplomas still gets me a little emotional. Graduation is why school districts exist. It's the magnum opus of K-12 education.

In today's world, however, school boards aren't all butterflies, roses, and diplomas. You don't have to search the internet for long to find videos filled with upset community members demonstrating how controversial school board meetings can be. And these long, charged meetings turn many good people away from service on school boards. And, believe me, I get it. I've sat through three hours of public comment, listening to community members dress me down because of nothing but a rumor. But that's a story for a different day.

Parents can be protective of their children, and rightly so, which is why there can be so much emotionally-charged rhetoric surrounding schools and districts. Strong leaders understand the gravity and responsibility of their decisions, weigh them carefully, and work hard to ensure success, which is why having strong leaders on school boards is critically essential.

As you can see from the first sentence of this book, this isn't a shortcut to fame or other political office, and it won't always be easy. Being a strong and effective leader is a lonely road. Although I can't say I haven't had my ten seconds of fame on multiple occasions. As the adage goes, all press is good press, right? But joking aside, despite what the public sees or thinks, public service is hard, meaningful work. Understanding and implementing this framework will make the job easier. I've used it to earn the respect of each organization I've served. Gaining the respect of those you work with is the only way to govern effectively.

But gaining respect doesn't mean you must do what the administration suggests. It doesn't mean you have to agree with them. It doesn't mean you can't push back, direct them to do something different, and overturn trends. On the contrary, it means you're obligated to hold each district leader accountable to the governing board's tenets and values. Values-Based Governance is a mechanism for holding boards and administrations accountable to those they serve.

Background

You might ask yourself, "Why is this guy writing a book about Governance? He started the book talking about being booed and harassed by people." It's a great question. I have asked myself the same question many times before writing the first word. However, the best books about leadership are messy and filled with failures and lessons learned. This book is no different, as the content draws on a decade of experience, most of which was devoted to educational governance.

My first board experience was helping start a school in our community. It is a small PK-8 program with around 650 students today. My friend asked me to join the effort when it was just four parents from the community sitting around a table in someone's dining room. My oldest kid had just turned two, and my wife asked me, "Why would you join this? Our kids probably won't go there." And my response was, "Because I believe we need a new school in our community." I had no idea what this "board" thing meant, but I have always seen education as a cornerstone for a prosperous, civil society. I decided to join the effort to further education and give back to our community.

After nearly five years on the board of the school I helped found, I ran and won a seat on our local school board for a four-year term. While on the district board, I worked with people from every side of nearly every spectrum: political, religious, age, creed, race, etc. The most unexpected and interesting phenomenon I've witnessed is how much criticism and outrage can come over extremely benign and uninteresting topics (I'm looking at you, bus schedules).

Shortly after being elected to our school board, I sought and received an appointment to a five-year term on our local public library board. My tenure was during a period when our library district was experiencing reduced funding, and book challenges were running rampant across the country (this coincided with my time on the school board). These were turbulent times, to be sure, but they were all manageable with the teams I had with both organizations.

I was elected president of each board I served on. Understand that election to the board presidency doesn't necessarily speak to leadership, though colleagues and the administration asking me to continue as board chair for additional terms does speak to leadership in that role.

I don't mean to make it sound easy because it wasn't. Remember that I was on the school board during an era of societal angst. All three organizations mentioned above had their share of choppy waters. What made the difference was how we navigated the challenges as they presented themselves, and that we kept our actions and words aligned with our values. Consistency and intentionality were key.

Leadership is doing the right thing, especially when it's hard. I coined this phrase to encourage my fellow leaders and friends to keep their values at the forefront and continue leading from a principle-driven perspective. It's a mantra about maintaining integrity and consistency, regardless of what issues arise on your board. I'll repeat it throughout the book, as I have to my fellow board members, to keep you focused during this journey.

Accomplishments

Looking back, each organization I served was made better—not by me, but because of the values-based leadership philosophy I brought with me. The accomplishments claimed and discussed in the following pages are those of the organization and the board collectively, not mine. In fact, as a board member, I can't do anything. In my role as board president, all I can do is lead. The rest of the board and the organization is where action takes place.

Only the board can make decisions, enact policy, and direct leadership to act. At the same time, the board doesn't do anything other than make decisions and hold the administration accountable for their actions. As board members, we don't teach or coach. We don't hire or fire. We don't manage lunch rooms or assist with carpool lines. Anything done in an organization is done by the leadership team and the staff working to make a difference every day. Put another way, the board can't implement its policies without the support of the administration and leadership teams.

Despite discussing the lack of personal accolades and abilities, I did have individual accomplishments while on each of my boards. I can look back at my time on each board and point to specific situations where I made a difference. Each instance has a common thread of accomplishment that ties them all together.

What I accomplished was championing values. I pushed my boards and aligned them with the organization's mission. I empowered our leadership teams to make strategic changes. I supported a culture of accountability. That's where you, as an individual board member, can make a lasting impact on the organization.

Comments About This Book

I learn by reading; part of that process is making marks in my books. I usually keep a highlighter and a pen next to my reading chair just for this purpose. Please do that here. This book is formatted with extra margin space to make it easy

Introduction

to read, take notes, and highlight what you want to reference. This book contains strategies you'll need to read through a few times before implementing them. That's okay. Making notes and dog-earing pages throughout this book will make it easier for you to go back and remember later.

To help from a cognitive perspective, each chapter includes a summary at the beginning. These short summaries prepare your brain for the information you're going to consume, and they help you process and organize the presented material.

Additionally, each chapter in the first three parts contains a "homework" section, which includes questions to help you process the information in each chapter and start thinking about how to apply the information contained in this book. There's no use in reading a book if you don't process it, understand it, and begin to relate it to your situation.

And with that, let's go ahead and get started.

Values-Based Governance In Practice

By now, you're probably thinking: 'Okay, but what does this actually look like?' That's the right question. Most frameworks start with theory, build on principles, and eventually get to practice. This book follows that path too, but first, I want to show you what Values-Based Governance (VBG) looks like in action. These snapshots will give you a concrete sense of the transformation ahead and help you understand why the foundational work in Part I matters. To that end, I want to express one of my values to you: Schools should be neutral environments, free of distractions, so that students can focus on learning.

The Philosophical Dilemma

You may not understand why this statement would be controversial, but I assure you it is. For controversy to exist, there must be (at a minimum) two opposing sides. The natural opposite of "neutral classrooms" would be "biased classrooms;" however, not many people would advocate for bias-filled or distraction-ridden classrooms.

To make an argument in favor of non-neutral classrooms, proponents give "biased" classrooms a more palatable name, which is where the phrase "intellectual freedom" originates. Let me state up front that I am a strong advocate for true intellectual freedom. Unfortunately, education has co-opted this concept.

You see, the term "intellectual freedom" is hard to argue against. To foster civil discourse (something else I'm passionate about), we must have the freedom to learn, study, and think about things in different ways. There must be freedom to investigate, learn, and draw differing conclusions for us to disagree civilly.

Without true intellectual freedom, we'd be subject to groupthink. We'd remain trapped in centuries-old thinking about problems. I would argue that without intellectual freedom, we wouldn't have inventors and thought leaders like Nikola Tesla, Thomas Edison, Albert Einstein, or Steve Jobs. Smartphones, cars, and light bulbs wouldn't have crept across the globe as they have. I believe that society would remain in a pre-Industrial Revolution without this concept of true intellectual freedom.

Unfortunately, intellectual freedom, especially in today's education system, is being used to promote controversial ideas to students. Exercising intellectual freedom gives staff members a license to introduce new ideas and topics that students may never have considered or encountered. By redefining "intellectual freedom," it becomes a guise for hanging political signs and religious icons on classroom walls, depriving students of the opportunity to choose their own adventure.

Despite how "intellectual freedom" sounds, the way public schools implement it is the exact opposite. Rather than allowing exploration, it becomes a restricted, predetermined path based on a staff member's beliefs. It's a stifled approach that can make students uncomfortable and create barriers to learning within the classroom.

And to be clear, this isn't purely political or religious. I've seen this with rock-and-roll bands, artwork, and many other varieties.

The Problem

As I stated earlier, schools should be neutral environments, free of distractions, so that students can focus on learning. Full stop. My advocacy of neutrality isn't about restricting intellectual freedom—it's about protecting it for all students. Neutrality serves as a necessary guardrail, ensuring that every student can explore ideas freely, regardless of their personal beliefs or their teacher's displayed preferences.

Let's take a moment and reflect on what the students are experiencing. The following is an admittedly contrived example, but I've designed it as an emblematic, albeit extreme, example of the barriers created by the co-opted concept of intellectual freedom.

You wake up on Monday morning—the first day of school. You're finally in high school, a freshman, and you can't wait to see what this new chapter has in store. After climbing out of bed and getting ready to show off "the new you," you swoop by the kitchen for a quick grab-and-go breakfast as you run out to the bus stop. You can't be late on the first day of school.

Checking the schedule on your phone as you enter through the front doors, you see so many of your friends from previous years. Everyone is smiling (and a little nervous); today is full of anticipation. Your favorite class last year was English, and now it's your first period this morning.

Making your way down the hall, you look at the placards posted on every door. Each entryway is emblazoned with a different number, climbing slowly until you get to your first-period class. You glance down at the room number on your phone and check it against the schedule once more, and everything matches. Opening the door, you walk in and think to yourself, "...what is this?"

In utter shock, you look around the room, and each wall is painted black. Pictures are hanging in the back of the room, all featuring dark, traumatic images. You stand there, mouth agape, as you wonder if this is some sort of senior prank. Your eyes hurriedly bounce to find an authority figure to help you make sense of this, but you can't find any adults. The other students look just as unsettled as you feel.

Then, your teacher trudges into the classroom. Long, pitch-black hair. Black fingernails, eyeliner, lipstick. Every stitch of clothing is black, ripped, or both. The teacher opens their mouth and says, "Welcome to Language and Literature class. We will be discussing proper paragraph structure this morning."

« »

Now, returning to the present, consider these questions:

- What is this student feeling right now?
- How interested are they in listening to the teacher?
- What is the student's focus on?
- Can the student focus on sentence and paragraph structure, which is the topic of today's class?

When we bog down classrooms with unnecessary materials, students can't focus on the material. Not only is the classroom an environmental distraction, but there are also cognitive distractions and barriers. The above vignette is an example of "intellectual freedom." Still, you can replace the black walls and imagery with any other topic, sociopolitical issue, or anything else you want, and the result will be the same.

As teachers adorn their classrooms with subjects and topics they value, they increase the likelihood of isolating students. No joke, I've seen classrooms with posters of presidential candidates plastered on the walls. Consider what happens when that teacher has a student who's supportive of "the *other* candidate?" These biased artifacts create a natural conflict between the student and the teacher. It's an unnecessary classroom distraction that creates learning barriers.

Teachers must build rapport with their students to engage them in meaningful instruction. Students need to be willing to learn from their instructors. Don't let a false sense of "intellectual freedom" be a deterrent. Neutral classrooms can be the catalyst for removing these barriers to learning.

The Solution

Now, I promised you a practical demonstration of Values-Based Governance in this section. So far, I've presented the philosophical dilemma and the problem as they play out in schools across the country, and now here's where the practical, values-based solution comes into play.

Remember, schools should be neutral environments, free of distractions, so students can focus on learning, and I believe neutrality is a guardrail for intellectual freedom.

The push for neutral classrooms actually constructively supports intellectual freedom. It allows students to express their opinions without the pressure of performing or saying something the teacher might not like. I've heard from students who were concerned about grade retaliation because their teachers were overtly pushing a different opinion than the students' own.

I don't believe the teachers would have done that, but that's immaterial. The issue is that the student's perception of the teacher's actions got in the way of genuine discourse and exploration of intellectual freedom.

During a walkthrough with administration, my board had noticed that flags of all varieties were hanging in classrooms across the district. Because my board wanted to support teachers and help reduce barriers to learning, our district passed a policy stating that only the U.S. and state flags were allowed in schools. It was a step in the right direction of providing neutral classrooms where students could focus on reading, writing, rhetoric, and math. They could concentrate on diagramming sentences and reading Shakespeare rather than the banners staff members had previously displayed.

And because our board worked in partnership with the district administration on this policy, it was received well by our principals. Over three months, we received fewer than five comments on the new policy, and there were no news articles or media spotlights because it wasn't controversial. It was a non-issue, presented as a way to promote student success.

That's one example of VBG in action as it relates to embedding values into policy. Now, let's look at another example that's a constant bane for board members across the country.

On the Practical Side

One of the biggest complaints I've heard from both existing and potential school board members is the duration of board meetings. It's actually a consistent reason I hear as to why community members won't run for the school board. I totally get it. Sitting in meetings that run until 10 PM, 11 PM, or even 1 AM (yes, I've been there) is not only exhausting, but it's demoralizing, too.

You want to do a good job as a board member, and that's admirable. Most school board members do. When I start engaging with folks about meeting length, I always ask this question: Is it responsible to make decisions that impact all the students and teachers in your district, sometimes dealing with millions of taxpayer dollars, at 11 p.m.?

I'm not saying you can't do it, but if you're in hour six of a meeting, dinner has long-since passed, and you've got a big meeting at work the next day, are you in the right frame of mind to truly consider all the implications of the decisions you're making? Are you properly evaluating and interpreting test results?

My experience is that boards often save decisions for the end of meetings. When it's 10 or 11 PM, most of the board members I've worked with are ready to leave. Handling essential decisions at this hour actually quashes vital conversations and dialogue amongst the board. You have the obligation and responsibility to make big decisions. You owe it to the community to do your due diligence on any business brought before your board, and when meetings drag on, that becomes harder to accomplish (and less likely that all board members will do it, too).

Shorter meetings are more productive and provide better opportunities for school board members to make good, responsible decisions. Some people would say that they can't make the meetings shorter, as then they'd have to meet more often to get the work done.

That's not true.

The Impact

Using the principles of Values-Based Governance discussed in this book, I reduced our monthly meeting time from more than five hours to less than two hours, and reduced our bi-monthly meetings to 11 per year. That's nearly a 60% reduction in time spent in board meetings, and the only differences were how we structured our agendas and implemented VBG.

I discuss this process and how we accomplished that feat in a later chapter, so I won't go into much detail here.

However, I wanted to give you the hope up front that you can do the requisite work in this role without having to give up valuable time with your family. You can help students and be an efficient board member.

« »

As you can see from both examples—whether addressing complex philosophical questions or practical operational challenges—Values-Based Governance provides a clear framework for effective school board leadership. You identify your values, align your policies, and adapt your culture through modeled behaviors, accountability, and consistent language.

This framework isn't about shortcuts or magic bullets. It's about clarity, consistency, and keeping student success at the center of every decision. It works for contentious cultural issues and mundane operational problems alike.

This is the framework outlined in this book. This is the path to govern differently. Now, let's build the foundation that makes it work.

Part I:
The Foundation

In Part I, I'll go over core concepts to help with understanding throughout the rest of the book. These foundational ideas lay the groundwork before introducing the Values-Based Governance framework and building on it throughout the remainder of the book. The concepts we'll discuss in the following chapters are governance, values, and leadership challenges facing school boards across the country.

Chapter 1:
Introduction to VBG

Chapter Summary:

In this foundational chapter, you'll learn what Values-Based Governance (VBG) is and why it's essential for effective school board leadership. You'll discover how VBG transcends partisan politics by focusing on student outcomes, and you'll understand common misconceptions about values-based approaches. You'll also learn what's required to succeed with VBG—humility, tenacity, and genuine commitment to students—and see why this framework matters more than ever in today's educational climate. By the end, you'll have a clear definition of VBG and understand the journey ahead.

When I first joined the board of the school I founded, my first foray into governance, I worked hard to prove I could hold my own and that I belonged. As the youngest member of our board, I tried to impress my colleagues with my education, vocabulary, ideas, and intelligence. I tried to convince everyone, including myself, that I belonged in a leadership role. But the great irony is that I had it all wrong: my focus was on me.

Focusing on yourself is the opposite of good governance and good leadership. I was writing the "how-to" book to stroke my ego. Eventually, my mindset shifted, and I realized that instead of focusing on myself and trying to show everyone how much I knew, I needed to focus on the students, the mission, and the organization. Reality set in, and I began to gain clarity. I needed to focus on *values*.

I wish I could tell you about the moment it happened. This "aha" moment when the sun shone brightly, the clouds parted, and I had an out-of-body experience showing me a golden brick road. But it didn't quite happen that way. It was much more subtle.

In complete transparency, I made mistakes. I got frustrated. I said things I shouldn't have said to people who didn't deserve the verbal assault. I also said things to people who deserved it. Despite being cathartic, it didn't accomplish anything. It hurt my reputation and made it harder for me to reach the end goal. More importantly, it wasn't professional behavior, and it wasn't becoming of my position. It took me time to understand how to navigate my role on the board and learn how to govern effectively.

The following framework helps you fast-track your education, audit a few life choices, learn from your mistakes, and quickly wield Values-Based Governance. It's an incredible tool. The goal of this book, and to a greater extent, this framework, is to decrease the time it takes you to become an effective member of your board.

Beyond Partisanship

Values-Based Governance is not about partisanship, despite what you may have seen, heard, or read about me and my motivations. I worked hard to ensure every vote I cast was in the best interest of the students in our schools and their education, the parents of those students, the teachers in our district, and the taxpayers who fund our educational system.

These decisions weren't always easy. I wrestled with making the right decisions. I spoke to people on my board and in my circles. With the diverse perspectives in our district, the board's decisions often conflicted with one or more stakeholder groups. I had to figure out how to reconcile the available options and make a decision, even though I knew the outcome might help one group while harming another.

You have to hold to your value system and decide how best to accomplish the district's mission and vision. School board members must determine what is in the best interest of the students and how best to equip them and set them up for academic success. As we'll discuss in a future chapter, Values-Based Governance provides a framework for making these decisions.

Many new board members assume school challenges require political solutions. In reality, most district issues are operational, cultural, or resource-based, not partisan. Academic achievement doesn't care about your political affiliation. Students struggling with reading need evidence-based literacy instruction, not ideological debates.

I've worked with board members across the entire political spectrum who were equally committed to student success. The ones who succeeded focused on outcomes; the ones who failed got trapped in political theater.

One of my proudest moments was when a community member who'd initially opposed me told a colleague, "I don't agree with his politics, but I trust him to do right by our kids." That's the power of Values-Based Governance; it transcends partisan divides by focusing on shared commitment to student success.

Values-Based Governance 101

First, we'll define Values-Based Governance to provide context for the rest of the book:

> *an approach to leading and stewarding an organization where decisions and actions are guided by core values, aligning personal, organizational, and stakeholder principles, aiming for ethical and effective management.*

This definition will be referenced in the following chapters, showing how the concepts and core tenets of VBG build on this foundation. Before continuing, go back and read that definition again, parsing it and relating it to your board members, interactions, votes, etc.

Misconceptions of VBG

As school boards have entered the limelight over the past few years, communities are paying attention to what's happening in district board rooms more than ever before. The reality is that this is a welcome byproduct. Parental involvement is a strong indicator of student success. But with that increased attention comes undue scrutiny.

No matter how many meetings someone shows up to, they're not going to be privy to all the information you have as a board member. Some of this scrutiny will focus on the board's decision-making and processes. Values-Based Governance is no exception. So, let's chat through some of the issues and misconceptions you might hear from well-meaning constituents.

Imposition of personal values. As discussed in Chapter 3, you need to consider values outside of your own. This consideration doesn't mean you give up your own convictions, but you can't keep such a myopic view of values during your time on the board. It's important to remember that the Founding Fathers wrote the Constitution to protect everyone, not just you. As a member of a school board, you're the government and must work to protect the rights of all students, parents, and community members.
Partisan politics by any other name. This chapter has already given you some insight into how this is a politic-agnostic framework. Your actions and decisions may be seen as partisan, especially because you must respond to laws enacted by partisan lawmakers. That doesn't mean VBG is partisan, or that you should be, but be prepared for community accusations.
Avoiding tough decisions. Some might see VBG as the board shirking its responsibilities and avoiding tough decisions. On the contrary, Chapter 4 will discuss how good ideas may be bad decisions for the board to make. Chapter 9 outlines how this framework allows decisions to be made as close to the problem as possible. It's about the right person making the right decisions.
Micromanagement of leadership. Chapter 10 discusses accountability within the district, ensuring leadership is making appropriate decisions. In fact, rather than feeling micromanaged, I've had superintendents thank their boards for doing the work of creating the foundational documents (Chapter 9), which gave them clarity and empowered them to respond to challenges and develop policy.
Quick fix solution. Proper change takes time, and implementing Values-Based Governance is no different. Defining who you are as an organization should be a process that involves your community. Then come policy changes and cultural adaptation, all of which the board must complete.

Even still, once all the official parts are in place, the process must continue with integrity. It will take multiple years to see the full benefits of your efforts.

Ego-driven efforts. It takes humility to make changes. The previous paragraph mentioned that this work will take multiple years, meaning some people on your board who start this effort won't be around to see it through. You can't care who gets the credit for the efforts here. The transition to VBG isn't about ego. It's about kids being successful. So, roll up your sleeves and make a difference.

What's Required to Succeed

Not every effort you and your board undertake will be successful, but VBG can buck that trend with the right formula. First, you need humility to acknowledge that your board needs to change how it operates. Next, you need the tenacity to stick to it when facing challenges, and finally, you need the patience to see this through to the end. Throughout all those phases, there are overarching perspectives and strengths required to fulfill your role on the board.

Genuine commitment to student outcomes. Committing to student outcomes must take preference over pushing personal or political agendas. The school board will fail your students if you allow those biases to influence your time on the board. VBG is a *genuine* commitment to students, which means you can't engage in mental gymnastics to justify how your decisions "benefit" students. Fulfilling this commitment includes having the courage to look constituents in the eye and make an unpopular decision when student interests are at stake.

Objective looks into district performance. Jim Collins, in his book *Good to Great*, states, "Good is the enemy of great." Good districts don't often have the motivation to change. Bad districts don't want to admit their actual performance. To engage in Values-Based Governance, you need to acknowledge where you are so that you can improve. Be willing to talk about the hard truths and the ugly data.

Willingness to learn from others. I stated earlier that this isn't an ego-driven effort. Whether ideas come from staff, administrators, community members, or students, you must acknowledge that you don't know everything. Seeking others' perspectives isn't a weakness. When serving a large district, how do you know what is happening in every classroom? Many board members were never educators, so overseeing curriculum puts them in unknown waters. Asking questions is a good start, but listening to answers is the only way to balance the equation.

Why VBG Matters Now

In the introduction, I painted a picture of the sheer magnitude of school board members needed in our country. Each one represents an opportunity to help our students and the next generation. Unfortunately, many of them are using their positions on the school board as a stepping stone to higher office. Board members focused on future roles can lead to board meetings stuffed with politics rather than focusing on student outcomes.

I've seen board members lose sight of why they're in this role and enjoy the limelight, leading them to grandstand on social media and reach out to local news outlets to highlight something innocuous. Some school board members check out when faced with an onslaught of angry community members, leaving the districts and the board in a defensive posture, where they're left to manage controversy rather than proactively shaping culture and instruction.

We're in a toxic cycle in which boards prioritize social issues over education, leading to back-and-forth control in subsequent election cycles.

There's an opportunity to stop this toxic cycle with the framework presented in this book. And here's the thing: when school boards function well, they can transform entire communities. I've seen it happen. Districts that implement strong governance frameworks see:

- Improved student achievement
- Higher staff retention and morale
- Increased community trust and support
- More effective use of taxpayer resources

That's not to say that everyone in your community will love you, because they won't. You'll still have opposition to sort out, but the key is that the rest of the community won't be listening to the noise. The social media posts get less traction. The local news stops reporting on every tip they get about your district. And you just might get a few folks who believe in what you're trying to accomplish.

A Preview of What's Coming Up

This book is structured to take you on a journey:

Part I (Chapters 1-4) builds your foundation. You'll understand what good governance looks like, how values work in practice, and the unique challenges facing school boards today.

Part II (Chapters 5-8) introduces the Values-Based Governance model. You'll learn the three core tenets—Strategic Alignment, Policy Development, and Cultural Adaptation—and how they work together.

Part III (Chapters 9-12) provides practical implementation strategies. You'll get tools, templates, and tactics for making VBG work in your specific context.

Part IV (Chapters 13-16) supplies key implementation tools, timelines, and troubleshooting guides to help you and your district successfully implement Values-Based Governance.

« »

Before diving into the framework itself, let's establish a common understanding of governance. Too many board members operate with incomplete or incorrect assumptions about their role. Chapter 2 will clarify what good governance actually looks like and why it matters for student success.

Remember: governance isn't about being important or having power. It's about being effective with the authority given to boards in the service of students who deserve your best efforts.

The journey toward Values-Based Governance starts with understanding the fundamentals of good leadership.

Homework – Chapter 1

1. Write down what you believe is the primary mission of a school board member. How does your current board's actual focus compare to this mission?

2. Review the "Misconceptions of VBG" section. Which misconception is your community most likely to have about principle-driven approaches? How would you address that concern?

3. From the "What's Required to Succeed" section, sincerely assess yourself: Which requirement (humility, tenacity, patience, genuine student commitment) will be most challenging for you personally? Why?

4. Think about your district's current challenges. How many of them are truly partisan political issues versus operational, cultural, or resource-based issues? What does this tell you about where your board should focus its energy?

5. What is one specific way you could demonstrate "genuine commitment to student outcomes over personal agendas" in your next board meeting or decision?

Chapter 2:
Framing Governance

Chapter Summary:

In this chapter, you'll learn what good governance actually looks like and see examples of common board dysfunction. You'll understand why accountability, leadership, and teamwork are essential, and see specific examples of how boards fail when they focus on ego, micromanagement, or conflict avoidance. By the end, you'll be able to identify whether your board practices good governance and know what changes to make.

When introducing any new framework or concept, building upon a foundation of shared knowledge and understanding is essential. Values-Based Governance (VBG) is no different, so the first building block is governance, as this framework equips you to govern and lead school districts effectively.

Looking back to our definition from chapter one, let's revisit the first part, as it directly speaks to the concept of governance. Definition (a):

> *an approach to leading and stewarding an organization where decisions and actions are guided...*

As a leader and a steward, your responsibility is to ensure the organization's longevity. The school district existed before you joined, and you need to ensure it will remain and continue serving students effectively long after you leave. The first hurdle in understanding Values-Based Governance—and subsequently wielding it appropriately—is understanding what governance is and how it works. This chapter will focus on good governance practices that span most philosophies and models because, in the end, good governance is good leadership.

Governance

Think about it this way: governance is leadership. However, this leadership role is a level of abstraction away from the typical leadership structure, as board members do very little management work. You're not always "in the building," but your authority is always present. Your decisions impact the entire district.

The conflict between management and governance is where things get odd and frustrating.

You don't supervise anyone. You don't decide to change the music played in the lobby or the weight of the paper the employees print on. You can't *do* many things. But you significantly influence everything in the district. It's an odd part about board governance: You have no authority as an individual board member, but the board (collectively) has all authority. In addition, the board is ultimately responsible for the organization's actions and outcomes.

Governance is the art of handling this dynamic productively. It's about influencing the organization without a direct managerial role. Finding an appropriate balance between personal desires and group authority can be hard, and VBG will help you distribute these needs appropriately.

Not all Governance is created equal, so let's spend a few minutes discussing the differences between good and bad governance.

Authority vs Power

I once met with a new board member who wanted to push through a controversial decision in her district. When I suggested the broader implications and some of the stakeholder concerns, she looked me dead in the eyes and said, "But we have the power to do this."

That hit me like a ton of bricks. The board member sitting in front of me wasn't thinking about service; she was thinking about power. She wanted the ultimate say and was willing to steamroll over community input and staff concerns simply because she could.

This mindset stands counter to effective governance, and understanding why it's a problem requires grasping the integral difference between *authority* and *power*.

Authority is your legal right to make decisions. As a school board, you collectively have the authority to hire and fire the superintendent, approve budgets, and set policy. You have the authority to vote 'yes' or 'no' on any issue that comes before the board.

Power, however, is about control and dominance. It's the desire to impose your desire regardless of consequences or stakeholder input. Power-seeking board members ask,

"How can I get my way?" rather than "What's best for students?"

At the center of this issue is the concept of the proper role of government, which is to serve those who elected you. You derive your authority from the consent of those who elected you. When you exert power, you're throwing that consent aside and foisting your own views on your community.

As an example of this dynamic, let me share an experience from my tenure as board president of our local district, when we were in the thick of book battles. We had parents who took exception to content in our libraries, and others who threatened lawsuits if we removed books from our collection. I'm not going to get into arguments for or against the books here, but rather demonstrate how we handled this issue from a Values-Based Governance perspective.

To set the stage, we were primarily talking about books in middle school libraries, as 6th graders and 8th graders span multiple developmental stages: social, emotional, mental, and intellectual, to name a few. The publisher classifies these books as young adult (YA), indicating that they are suited for readers aged 14 and older. The recommended age is notably older than that of typical 6th- and 7th-graders, and such content may not be developmentally appropriate for younger middle schoolers. This age rating reflects multiple factors, including potentially mature themes, language complexity, and conceptual sophistication that assumes more developed reasoning abilities.

As a board, we could have easily exerted our *power* over the community. Such power could have manifested in several ways. First, we could have said "all books are fair game" and made all the books available to all students. Taking this approach would have been a slap in the face of those parents pushing for a more modest, age-appropriate library collection. On the other hand, we could have unilaterally pulled questionable books from the library, which would have put us in a legal battle and removed access to some age-appropriate books based on arbitrary criteria.

Instead of either of those options, we decided to use the *authority* granted to us by the community to ensure parents could control the materials their students consume. We provided a new option during registration, which I affectionately call the George Strait Method, that forced parents to "check yes or no" by selecting either "yes, my kid can check out young adult materials" or "no, my kid cannot check out young adult materials." There was no default option, so all parents would have to make an active decision for each child.

In this way, our board was able to cede power back to the community that elected us. All parents were able to choose how their students would interact with our library content. Returning authority to the governed rather than taking an opportunity to exert power over them demonstrated our commitment to the proper role of local government.

I've seen power-hungry board members destroy district cultures, chase away talented superintendents, and create years of instability that directly harms student achievement. Board members who focus on accumulating and wielding power quickly become toxic to their organizations. They create adversarial relationships with staff, divide communities, and turn board meetings into political battlegrounds. Worst of all, they lose sight of why they're there in the first place: to serve students. They justify their actions as if having authority automatically makes their decisions right.

Values-Based Governance offers a different approach. Instead of asking "Can we do this?" you ask "Should we do this based on our mission, values, and commitment to student success?" Instead of seeking power over others, you seek influence through service, relationship-building, and consistent focus on outcomes.

Authority is a tool for service, not a weapon for control.

What is Good Governance

As was stated previously, good governance is good leadership. It's that simple. However, despite being simple, it's not as easy as it sounds. I've seen examples of both good and bad leaders during my time working on school boards. The good news is that we can identify specific practices required for good governance. These traits for good, effective governance are accountability, leadership, and teamwork. Despite many board members having held roles that require these traits, they are ineffective in governance because these traits manifest differently in a governance setting. This lack of effectiveness often stems from the need to act as a single unit.

In addition to the group dynamic, you, as the board, are not in the building 100% of the time. While serving as school board president at the district and the charter school, I spent an average of eight to ten hours in the office each month, outside of board meetings. When I wasn't the president, those hours dropped to a range of four to six. Most people agree that a mere 4 to 10 hours per month isn't enough time to lead an organization. And most people would be correct.

The need to spend time at the district's office to lead effectively holds true in the traditional understanding of leadership. Still, there is plenty of time to govern the organization when you adhere to good, Values-Based Governance practices.

Accountability

The first core trait of good Governance is accountability. Many folks have heard of "rubber stamp boards," where board members show up and approve whatever the district leadership asks them to, giving the administration a carte blanche "rubber stamp" of approval. There's no accountability between the board and the district. Rubber stamping is textbook bad governance.

The board must hold the district and its leadership accountable to ensure the administration performs its duties with fidelity. Accountability doesn't just happen because you want it to. The board must set specific, clear expectations to share across the organization. Accountability can't exist without clear expectations.

In many cases, these expectations will come from governing policy, which aligns with the organization's foundational documents, such as its mission, vision, and values. These records must align with the goals and expectations provided by the governing board.

"Strategic alignment" occurs when the mission, vision, goals, values, and policy align. This utilization of strategic alignment is the most efficient and effective way to establish accountability measures. Although it can be tedious and require many changes, once your organization has achieved strategic alignment, the superintendent, leadership team, and each staff member will know the district's expectations.

However, having these expectations listed clearly and specifically is only part of accountability. The real work is to make sure the organization meets the stated expectations. There's a saying, "You get what you inspect, not what you expect." So, the other side of the accountability coin is inspection.

Whatever policy methodology you use in your district, it's critically important to establish consistent checkpoints with your superintendent to ensure their focus stays on the right things. In sports, the ball follows your focus. When you're playing catch in the backyard, you will miss your target if you turn to look at the dog as you release the ball.

It's the same principle in governance. You have to give the most attention to your intended target. In a school district, this should be academics.

We'll explore strategic alignment, the foundational documents, and the practical side of accountability later in the book.

Leadership

I will echo a phrase introduced in Chapter 1, "Leadership is doing the right thing, especially when it's hard." I'm starting the leadership section with this phrase because it's essential to keep it accessible in your short-term memory. I continually remind board members of this phrase because it's easy to say feel-good things. It's easy to make people happy. It's easy to maintain the status quo. It's easy to do the easy thing. However easy is not leadership.

I like watching HBO's *Band of Brothers*. I've seen it several times, and I'll watch it several more. It's a great lesson on leadership. World War II was a difficult time in human history, and many young men found themselves in challenging situations. The *Band of Brothers* show follows a group of soldiers during their time in Europe. After their commanding officer abandoned them, headquarters selected one of the men to lead the team because of the respect he had earned from the men around him.

The young officer cared deeply about his team, and the story arc chronicles the hard decisions he had to make. He put his team in difficult situations, resulting in many of them dying. They had a mission to accomplish, and they all worked together to meet the call.

Whenever his team had a difficult mission to accomplish, this young, freshly minted officer was right beside them. His willingness to fight alongside his team led to several promotions until he could no longer go on missions with his men. At one point, he even defies the general's orders to send his team on a suicide mission. The story goes

Framing Governance

that the commanding officer held his troops that night and sent a fabricated report. His willingness to risk his career saved many of his men's lives.

Board decisions rarely involve life and death, but you'll likely have to put your team in uncomfortable situations to work towards your mission. When you focus on the objective, your mission, and your vision, the decisions become easier, even if the execution and ramifications aren't easy.

There are volumes (and perhaps even full libraries) dedicated to leadership. I don't have enough pages in this book to fully detail leadership, but I will discuss the topic more throughout the remaining pages. For now, suffice it to say, "Leadership is doing the *right* thing, especially when it's hard."

Teamwork

Effective leadership requires teamwork. A leader without a team leads no one—they become an inspiration only to themselves. Even with a team, you, as a leader, must be willing to walk through hardship with them. Remember, doing the right thing can be (and likely will be) difficult, and if you make a decision that affects your team and then walk away, leaving them to do all the heavy lifting, you're no longer a leader—you're a dictator. Leadership requires teamwork.

As board members, you can't afford to be dictators. Remember, as a board, you can't *do* anything without the superintendent and other district leaders. Once you walk out of the board meeting, your part is over. You lose respect and influence within the organization if you make decisions that put your team in turbulent waters and leave them to fend for themselves. Your board must be willing to step up to the plate as teammates, share the responsibility, and continue the march towards success.

One of the governing boards' responsibilities is to approve budgets. One board I began working with had not passed a balanced budget in several years. The board was dipping into reserves every year to make ends meet. When I asked why the board had handled the budget so irresponsibly, I was told, "What else are reserves for than to use them?" I wish this were a work of fiction, but it's not.

In the first year of my involvement, the initial budget presented to the board showed expenses 30% higher than revenues. For those who aren't "math" people, the district projected spending $130 for every $100 it received. Overspending by that margin was unacceptable, obviously. The next budget, a candidate for approval, was only 8% over budget. I reminded the board about their duty to be responsible stewards of taxpayer dollars. The board, as a whole, agreed and told the district to work towards a balanced budget over a 2-year cycle. After much discussion, the board permitted a 2% budget overage for the current cycle, requiring a balanced budget by the following year.

Requiring balance was a significant change in the right direction. The district's finance team had already done a lot of work to get from 30% to 8%, and it was necessary to acknowledge the work the finance team and leadership had already completed. Once the meeting was over and the board had reached consensus on the 2% threshold, the other board members left the building, but I offered to sit down with the leadership team and go through the budget line by line to help make hard decisions.

Knowing this would impact many staff, I was willing to shoulder the blame and responsibility for cutting programs or positions, if needed, to ensure the leadership team could maintain its influence and standing with the rest of the district. I knew when facing hardships, it was incumbent upon leaders to roll up their sleeves, jump into the trench, and help the team meet the goal. Even if my offer had been turned down (which it wasn't), I knew I had shown that I was a team player. I wasn't asking the team to do something I wasn't willing to do, even when it was hard and uncomfortable. Or, *especially* if it's hard and uncomfortable.

My willingness to be a teammate marked a turning point in my relationship with the leadership team. It wasn't my role to sit and confer with the administration and finance team to comb through the budget outside the board meetings. Going line by line through the budget like that is operational rather than governance-focused. I recognized this discrepancy, but I offered to sit down with the team and get the hard stuff done. And it was the only time I made such an offer. The board had set the expectation, and the leadership team knew I had their backs.

You're not a leader if you don't have a team behind you. Ensure the team is with you so you don't look like a lunatic running into battle alone.

What Good Governance Isn't

Since I've discussed the three primary facets of good governance, let's discuss what good governance isn't. The simplest way to describe it is to say it's the opposite of the above, but that would be an oversimplification. Instead, I'll explain bad governance by defining four types of dysfunction, which align with our previously listed leadership types: The Narcissistic Tyrant, The Well-Meaning Do-Nothing, and the Values-Based Leader. The Values-Based Leader has been described previously in the "What Good Governance Is" section, so we'll focus on the other two types below.

For each of the four dysfunctions detailed below, I'll provide generalized examples from experiences I've had, followed by a quick explanation about why they're good examples of bad governance. Gender is alternated in the examples below to help maintain anonymity.

The Stair-Stepper

Leaders need to be humble. You're not important as an individual on a school board because your authority comes only from the board's majority vote. If you don't have at least two other friends (totaling three votes on a five-person board), your opinion is just that: your opinion. There's nothing actionable. I knew a board member once who bragged about her role on the board. She wore her name tag everywhere she went and always pumped out her chest when she walked into the boardroom (or any other room, for that matter). She was important because she was a board member. There was no humility in her actions or her demeanor.

"Board meetings should be held often and last a long time," was her unspoken mantra. Sitting behind the dais, on camera, demonstrated her importance to the community. This board member wanted everyone to know her opinions mattered and made sure people heard them, repeating them when folks didn't listen. She would cut back-room deals with other board members to push her ideas through. Reputation was the only thing she cared about. She wanted to solidify her importance to safeguard her reputation and ensure it persisted beyond her term.

This dysfunction type, The Stair-Stepper, sees their board "service" as a stepping stone to bigger and better things. Ego and ambition are the key motivators for the "Stair-Stepper" dysfunction. It doesn't mean they're moving on to other political positions, though often that's the case. Their board seat could simply be for other community organizing, to support a business/podcast, elicit donations for a non-profit, or anything else where the community attention helps drive their personal ambitions.

Our example above missed the point of public *service*, focusing only on herself and what this role could do for *her*.

In the paraphrased words of President Kennedy, "Ask not what your district can do for you—ask what you can do for your district." When board members already have their vision on new endeavors, they lose sight of the current task.

They lose sight of the students, the parents, the teachers, and the community they were elected to serve.

The Stair-Stepper often believes that specific rules and expectations don't apply to them. I've seen board members disregard board agreements and conduct policies. When called out, they act offended—how dare anyone question their judgment or integrity? After all, they're elected board members.

This sense of entitlement extends to accountability measures. The Stair-Stepper expects staff and administration to follow every policy to the letter while exempting themselves from those same standards. This double standard damages the board's credibility and undermines its ability to hold others accountable.

All of the above demonstrates a gross misunderstanding of what matters. Caring for the students in your community matters. Having a strong culture where teachers want to work matters. Increasing taxpayer confidence in the district matters. Ego does not (and will never) matter. Remember, your "importance" as a board member only exists because of the people you serve. Maintaining your focus on students rather than yourself goes back to that whole "consent of the governed" concept from high school civics. Without the students or the voters, there's no position or authority.

The only "important" things are remembering the district's mission and student success, and ensuring sustainability for the future.

The Crusader

Community engagement is a key component of good governance and board work. After all, you work for the people; why not engage them? One board member I worked with took this to an extreme. No issue was too big or too small. If a community member engaged with an issue, this board member took it upon himself to resolve it.

These campaigns would continue for weeks or sometimes months. The board would need to address more important matters related to student outcomes, but he would repeatedly bring up some random issue. Due to its regularity and repetition, it became a running joke among the other board members.

This cycle of fake heroism was problematic for several reasons. The first and most apparent was that the board member focused more on his own goals than on the district's mission. He neglected his duty to all the staff, students, and parents in his district to make himself feel and look good. Along those same lines, he chose minor issues that affected only a handful of people and raised them as his standard, informing the public about his unnecessary fight.

Another way The Crusader manifests is through grandstanding, which is blowing something out of proportion for the sake of drawing attention. The impetus of this grandstanding could be one's own values, a group's values, or simply for the sake of obstructing the work. Think "prima donna" on the stage of local government. Rarely does this obstructionist behavior actually benefit students and their academic journeys, but it always draws attention to The Crusader.

The most toxic manifestation of The Crusader involves weaponizing rules and policies against fellow board members. They'll make up creative interpretations of policies and publicly attack colleagues during board meetings, sometimes even orchestrating coordinated campaigns with community allies to discredit or force out other board members. The irony is often palpable—board members who preach about civility and anti-bullying while actively bullying their colleagues in the name of their cause.

Board members must have trust within their team. The Crusader destroys that trust by prioritizing political battles over student outcomes, fighting to prove their superiority and resolve rather than focusing on the district's mission.

All of the theatrics boils down to "making mountains out of molehills" energy. These board members prevent the board from addressing bigger issues by weaponizing a set of values—either their own or a group's. In many cases, the board's work must take a back seat to The Crusader's whims. Allowing a Crusader to control the board's priorities will present an unfocused, scattered front to the public. It will also prevent the board from doing the necessary work owed to their district and community.

The Crusader often envisions themselves as the picture of justice, fighting for those they believe are underserved. The "fight" they tout is a guise to prevent the board from focusing on something else, which is why you need to focus entirely on student outcomes. It makes others look silly when they grandstand against something that will objectively help students succeed.

You don't have to be a Crusader; simply be a good board member.

The Hands-on Hero

Managers and leaders are two different words for a reason. While managers do, leaders empower. This distinction is significant because, as board members, your job is to lead. Management is the job of the administration.

One board I worked with had a board member who took it upon herself to manage the district rather than lead. She struggled to understand the difference. Whenever the board discussed business items during a meeting, she would want to sit down with the district's leadership team to develop an implementation plan. She wanted regular status meetings and updates, often stopping by the district's office to meet with the superintendent and other key personnel.

With the best of intentions, this board member would walk through different school buildings to gather feedback from students, teachers, and volunteers. She would meet with parents regularly to solicit their opinions and ideas. Without fail, those meetings would evolve into new district-level initiatives, which she would try to oversee. She acted as though she wanted to be employed by the district rather than lead it.

When the administration didn't implement her suggestions quickly enough, she would escalate. She'd tell staff that if they didn't want to follow her recommendations, she'd get the board to vote on new policy changes and force implementation. The manipulation of staff created tension between the board and administration, undermining the partnership that effective governance requires. The superintendent and leadership team found themselves managing around this board member rather than working with the whole board.

The issue here can be subtle. Many new board members might think this lady was doing her job by working to resolve issues raised by students and parents. But remember: good governance is leadership, not management. It wasn't that this board member had ill intent, but the way she interjected herself into the district's operation, outside of the board's majority, was the problem. If she had brought issues up during a board meeting for a complete discussion, things would have been smoother, but she wanted the credit and to do the work herself.

As an individual board member, your role isn't to force anything or manage implementation. If someone finds themselves having to push their ideas onto staff, they should pause and ask themselves, "Why?" They're likely trying to shoulder work that isn't under their purview. Step back, talk to the board president, and try to refocus.

Leadership is the *why*, and management is the *how*. The board member here was too involved in the how rather than the why. She was trying to be a Hands-on Hero, rather than a board member.

The Appeaser

Boards are ultimately accountable for the district's budget, results, and reputation. So, it's easy for board members to slip into the false role of "babysitter leadership." For example, fighting is unacceptable at my house. My wife and I intervene quickly when voices rise, sending everyone to their corners and refocusing the kids on something more productive. Babysitters handle this differently. When the kids start to fight, they give them a snack and put them in front of the television.

It's hard to enforce rules when you're not always present. Babysitters are only present for a short time, and my kids even admitted they intentionally make it hard for babysitters at bedtime (my sincerest apologies if any of you are reading this). They don't want to go to bed, and they know the babysitter won't fight very hard. They're only here briefly; my wife and I will return and restore order. It's difficult for babysitters to hold our kids accountable in the long term, so they move into "appeaser" mode and do whatever it takes to survive. They want to survive and babysit another day.

In this way, I had a board member who fell into this "babysitter leadership" style, where he just tried to get everyone working together long enough to survive. He didn't want conflict. He metaphorically handed out lollipops and turned on a show to distract everyone. The board member displayed these "babysitter" tendencies with other board members, staff, and the broader community. He just wanted to appease everyone—go along to get along. It was incredibly ineffective.

When you, as the board of education, are responsible for accountability, you can't simply appease everyone to move past problems. Even though you're in your role for only a short time, you must keep the district, the culture, the results, and the budget moving toward the mission. In school districts, your four-year stint on the board could cause lasting harm to students if your focus is on appeasing rather than effective governance.

Placating the district and community plays directly into the "rubber stamp" board we've discussed previously. When you have an Appeaser on the board, they want to reduce conflict and move on. This aversion to conflict often manifests as a refusal to question the administration or others who bring forward information. Poking and prodding can be seen as low-trust activities, so they approve what the district wants to limit friction (or the appearance of friction).

This Appeaser dysfunction can also stem from the belief that the board member is unqualified to question the administration. "They're the professionals, so why would I think I know better than them?" is an oft-heard phrase, but it's the wrong mentality. The reality is that you're on the board as an accountability measure from the community. Part of your qualification is that you're not an education expert, and you don't have to be.

Asking questions isn't about questioning motives or snooping around to have some "gotcha" moment. It's about everyone coming together to help students grow. You're on the same team. Iron sharpens iron, and so does asking questions. Checks and balances are a necessary part of government.

Don't despise conflict, but make sure it's constructive. Constructive conflict leads to growth.

Navigating Dysfunction

The first three dysfunctions listed above—The Stair-Stepper, The Crusader, and The Hands-on Hero—are active issues, in which board members are actively doing work that's antithetical to the board's desired outcomes. The fourth dysfunction—The Appeaser—is a passive type of dysfunction in which the district (or activist groups) can throw its weight around and determine the outcome.

All of these are problematic, as you can see. These dysfunctions make it nearly impossible for the district to work towards its mission and vision. Limiting these behaviors can become a full-time job.

Unfortunately, there's no silver bullet here. It takes time and intentional effort to bring attention to these dysfunctional behaviors and start seeing improvement. The first step is to build relationships with these board members. Take them to coffee or meet them before a board meeting. Work to understand what their motivation is for being on the board.

Later in this book, we'll discuss strategies for developing a shared values statement, a powerful tool for refocusing dysfunctional board members and reorienting them toward the board's purpose.

Just remember, many of these dysfunctions are ego-driven, so grandstanding at board meetings or publicly censuring them won't be very effective. Build relationships. Redirect to values. Model the appropriate behaviors. Utilizing these strategies will help you win the long game.

Why Good Governance is Important

Since we've seen some examples of bad governance, let's discuss why good governance matters. Good governance matters because it's effective. Let's look at a few of the themes from the previous vignettes.

First is the theme of selfishness. Good governance focuses on the district rather than the individual board members. Keeping the organization's mission and vision at the forefront is a sure way to maintain your focus. Problems arise when board members elevate themselves over the district and the students. It becomes especially harmful when multiple board members take this selfish perspective. This form of ego generates conflict, as each board member tries to outshine and outperform the others, proving they're the board's best and most altruistic members. Such jockeying is often rooted in insecurity and in the desire to prove they belong. Ultimately, it harms the organization, the students, and the staff you were elected to serve. Leadership is selfless, but this is purely selfish.

The second big theme is improper focus. In a few stories above, board members focused on the wrong things. Focusing on the wrong things doesn't necessarily mean those things weren't important; it simply means they weren't the proper place to spend the board's time and energy. These members focused on minor issues with limited impact on the community or on operational items, telling the administration how to solve problems rather than focusing on the *"why"* behind the issues. Again, keeping your eye on the goal will do wonders for effectiveness as a board and an organization.

The third prominent theme to consider is undermining the team. Teamwork helps keep everyone on the same page and requires trust, which the behaviors in the vignettes above eroded in multiple ways. Trust is a central ingredient to a successful team. Successful teams are effective in progressing toward the district's mission and vision. Remember, good governance requires teamwork, and when the team isn't working together, your students and stakeholders are the ones who lose.

The last theme to notice is the lack of accountability. When board members avoid conflict and rubber-stamp decisions to keep the peace, there's no real accountability happening. But there is a larger accountability issue at hand. Let me ask a question. How can you hold someone accountable for 15 different priorities? In several of the dysfunctions above, board members jumped from issue to issue without establishing coherent goals to hold their superintendent and leadership team accountable. For accountability to exist, the board has to set clear, specific goals. When the board works on whims as they arise, there's no way to achieve sufficient clarity.

Good governance is essential for effective leadership. It keeps the mission and vision in plain view and works to improve the well-being of students, staff, parents, and the broader community.

Homework – Chapter 2

1. Reflect on when you witnessed or experienced poor governance practices on a board or in an organization. What specific behaviors or dynamics contributed to the ineffective governance? How could the board have approached its duties differently to fulfill them more effectively?

2. As a board member, how would you establish a culture of accountability within your district? What specific policies, procedures, or mindsets would you work to instill to ensure the administration is meeting the board's expectations?

3. Imagine you are in a situation where you strongly disagree with the majority of the board on an important decision. How would you navigate that tension while upholding your responsibilities as a team player and advancing the district's mission? What strategies could you use to influence the decision constructively?

4. Describe a time when you had to make a difficult decision as a leader that went against the preferences of specific stakeholders. How did you approach communicating and implementing that decision? What insights did you gain about the balance between doing "the right thing" and maintaining positive relationships?

5. How about assessing governance's overall health and effectiveness within your school board or organization? What metrics or indicators would you use to determine whether the board practices sound governance principles such as accountability, leadership, and teamwork?

Chapter 3:
Defining Values

Chapter Summary:

In this chapter, you'll explore the different types of values that influence board decisions: personal, organizational, societal, and group values. You'll learn how these value systems interact and sometimes conflict, and understand why staying true to your values while considering others is crucial for effective governance. By the end, you'll know how to navigate competing value systems and use decentralization to embed values throughout your district.

Now that we've discussed good governance and the first block of the Values-Based Governance foundation is firmly in place, we need to start building our second foundational block: values. Again, we will begin this chapter by reviewing the relevant part of our definition from the first chapter. The second part of the Values-Based Governance definition is as follows:

...guided by core values, aligning personal, organizational, and stakeholder principles...

Values are the underlying rationale for why we make the decisions we make and do the things we do. These values could be anything. We've carried some of these values since childhood and developed others over time.

Below are a few examples of how your values influence your decision-making.

- You might value customer service over food quality, so you choose restaurants with friendlier wait staff, even though the food isn't exceptional.
- You might value environmental friendliness more than horsepower, so you choose your vehicle accordingly or use a bicycle as your transportation.
- You might value parental choice in education over control, so you offer specific options at your school or invite charter school applications to provide those parent-led opportunities.

The above are just a few examples of how values impact the decisions we make every day. When you're sitting on a school board, there will be many circumstances where you'll have to make hard decisions, and it will be incumbent upon you to use your values to make those decisions wisely. The application of your values can relate to anything from purchasing curriculum to tax initiatives or approving agreements with third-party vendors. In nearly every case, the district has a specific outcome in mind. But *you* have to make the decision. That's why you're on the board, to begin with.

The dichotomy between your values and the district's desired outcomes is where things get a little complicated. You have to be able to take what the superintendent and the administration are telling you, view it through the lens of the district's expectations and desired outcomes, and make a decision that aligns with your value system. You need to be able to sleep at night, and making principle-based decisions is my best advice for you.

So, let's discuss the different types of values and how they impact the decision-making process.

Types of Values

More important than having values is being able to identify them. You need to know why you make the choices you make. Understanding these drivers is an integral step in Values-Based Governance. To help you identify these values, I'm defining five value sets to consider: your values, your board's values, the district's values, societal values, and group values.

Your Values. Your values are simply that: *your* values. These values build your paradigm, and they're how you justify what you do, consciously or subconsciously. Your values are often tightly held, and when attacked or questioned, they can leave you unsettled, as they are core to who you are. Oftentimes, parents, mentors, or other close individuals pass them down to you. Sometimes, we develop values to contrast the examples set before us. Regardless of how we form them, they stick to us closely and are almost a default position.

Board Values. Just as you have your own set of values, the other members you serve with each have their own. Sometimes they overlap; sometimes they don't. Often, there is common ground, but conflict is apt to arise when these value systems differ. Focusing on shared values is important because it helps you reach consensus as a board. We spent an afternoon creating a shared values statement on one of my boards, which served as a frame of reference for the superintendent and us during discussions, decision-making, and navigating policy work.

District Values. The district's values can be hard to determine. It amalgamates different views, opinions, and values over time. This mash-up isn't just from the board members who have led the district; the organization integrates societal and group values over time. These district values get muddled over time, partly because of the nature of these entities' long-term existence and the fact that board members regularly rotate in and out. Every time a new board member is added or removed, you have a whole new board, which creates new dynamics in how the district's value system gets implemented and interpreted.

Societal Values. These are values held by society writ large. These are undercurrents sweeping across the nation, and as they influence an ever-increasing number of individuals, they begin to grow into larger waves, shaping value systems and policies. Once policy codifies these values, revision takes time—meaning outdated societal values from 20 years ago can linger in your policies today, creating problems as society's values continue evolving. For example, some societal values, such as those enshrined in the U.S. Constitution, are internalized by most Americans, which maintains them for long periods. However, others are only blips, lasting for a few months or years if they gain traction. Sticking to these value systems from a generation ago can result in deprecated policies despite those policies still being active and unchanged.

Group Values. Group values are often subsets of societal values. They typically come into play when activist groups, chambers of commerce, or even neighborhoods band together to fight a specific policy or issue. Often, the group only exists to get you, or your board, to support the values they represent. These values, which may or may not be best for the organization, typically represent a minority stake in the district. It's easy to get swept up in the emotions of helping those individuals, but you must keep your head about you. Board members who focus on group values rather than their own or the district's can lead to the "Crusader" pitfall discussed in the previous chapter.

« »

Knowing you're now in a principle-driven role, ask, "What values should you be focused on when implementing the VBG model?" Do you draw on your values while completely ignoring those of groups and the organization? Do you draw from the district's or society's values and leave your value system aside? The answer is a little bit of everything. Your decisions as a school board member are often too complex for a single reply. However, you must understand the dynamics and interplay among these value systems.

Interplay of Value Systems

You must be true to your values and convictions. You can't simply impose your values on others, because that will cause conflict and turmoil. When your values directly contradict the values of your fellow board members or the district, you will spend all your time fighting a battle that doesn't help the students you're there to serve. Misappropriated attention will create resentment among all stakeholders, both inside and outside the district. This conflict can result in the same guttural reaction as telling someone to "calm down."

And who do you think suffers the most from this? The students do. Those you're supposed to serve will be the biggest losers when the district's leaders fight amongst themselves.

When you get involved in such fights, attempting to convince others that *your* values are more important than *theirs*, it will hurt your reputation. It makes you look bad. You become a self-advocating martyr driven by ego and selfishness. To put it bluntly, the battles you wage and how you fight them reveal your character. Battling to belittle others and win some false sense of moral superiority demonstrates that your only concern is your own clout and social standing. Your beliefs are bigger and more important than theirs. Eschewing others' values is the quickest way to lose effectiveness rather than gain it because others will see you as a bully.

These discussions turn personal, as they often involve deeply held values. It's a difficult task to change people's minds on such fundamental tenets. However, focusing solely on society's value system will leave you without a voice altogether. The voters elected you for a reason.

Suppose all you do is sit at the dais and align with the current societal values. In that case, you should send out surveys and relinquish the board's decision-making authority to the broader community. Our forefathers set up a Republic rather than a Democracy for a reason. They understood representation, discourse, and the importance of individual values. Democracies allow 51% of a group to tell the other 49% what to do, called "tyranny of the majority." If boards focused solely on societal values, we could adopt a purely democratic process in our districts and let a simple majority decide outcomes for all district-level decisions. Allowing the community to vote on every district decision would drastically increase costs, as ballot initiatives aren't cheap.

Similarly, you can't focus too much on the district's values, or you'll repeat what they have always done. As we discussed, you will become a "rubber stamp" board, or "The Appeaser," if you will, which is bad governance. There's no point in having a board when this happens, since the

Defining Values

superintendent and leadership team could make all the district's decisions. As board members, it's incumbent upon you to critically process what the district administration is proposing. What the district presents to the board is born from the organization's value system. It's important for board members to consider these district values, but don't succumb to them.

Districts are all too aware of their values. This awareness can lead to protectionism by the organization. If the values they've espoused and advanced feel threatened by your value system, district leaders might cut you from the communication loop. I've seen this happen firsthand in a district I worked with. What was once a unified board became a board with one divergent member. Once that happened, the district leadership stopped communicating with that member outside of board meetings. Keeping this board member at arm's length resulted in a loss of impact, respect, and influence for the board and the district.

This misalignment between board and district values is problematic because the district would rather preserve its current values than change them. I encountered a similar situation in which most of the board changed soon after the district completed a new strategic plan. The new board's values no longer aligned with the district's strategic direction. The district's long-term goals eventually reflected the board's values, but it took nearly three years and a new superintendent to get there.

The difficulty in changing the district's values lies in the fact that those values are what drive day-to-day operations. It's how the leadership team knows what decisions to make and how to serve your students, staff, and parents. It's essential to keep this at the forefront of your mind. Forcing a shift in these values will have a ripple effect on how staff begin to implement policy throughout your district.

Finally, emphasizing group values will shove you into a corner, as you'll end up with different groups pushing mutually exclusive ideals, each expecting you to champion their specific value set. When you spend your time aligning with and supporting the values of these groups, you'll have to decide which group to support while dismissing the others. Most boards and districts have conflict-of-interest and anti-bribery policies. However, these policies don't stop groups from trying to influence leaders. It isn't always a substantial amount, and it isn't always monetary. Oftentimes, it's simply, "We'll come do this thing and support you if you vote our way." It's a classic quid pro quo scenario.

I've also seen groups try to sway board members to their values through guilt. "We helped you win your seat, so now you owe us." You can hear such a refrain nationwide, but this is a logical fallacy. Yes, it might be true, but it's not entirely accurate, as the specific activist group didn't hold enough votes to elect you. Their numbers might have helped push you over the edge, but it required many other community voters to elect you to your seat.

I can speak with authority on this issue as I've had my fair share of people pressuring me to vote a certain way. Groups have threatened lawsuits against me to prevent me from using a quote by a Founding Father during a board meeting. I've had even worse stuff happen because I did what I believed was right. And the push to conform to group values has come from both sides of the ideological spectrum, with activists and political groups alike applying pressure.

Despite their persuasive attempts, I have always stayed true to my core values. It hasn't always been easy, and being true to my value system led to all the nasty stuff from page one. In the end, I have to answer for my votes and be able to sleep at night. If I'm following someone else's value system, I must reconcile that deviation with my integrity.

Ultimately, prioritizing society's, the district's, or a group's values over yours in the ways above would be an abdication of your duties. Your role on the board is to make decisions. You spoke about your values during your campaign, and your community chose *you* to represent them. They voted for you because of your values.

But your values don't exist in a vacuum. The challenge is to stay true to your values while considering those of the district, group, or society. If you're not solid in your values, resolving these differences can cause internal friction. It can also cause problems if you're too entrenched. This conflict arises when you rely solely on your value system, disregarding those around you.

Whether voters supported you based on a single issue or your entire platform, they chose you over everyone else for a reason. You are now obligated to make decisions based on the value system that puts you in that seat. Simply following these other value systems alone is handcuffing you and your effectiveness. It also undermines the community's confidence in you. They believe you will use your best judgment and make decisions for the most significant benefit of your students and stakeholders. You need not disappoint them.

Activism vs. Governance

Your first job as a board member is to stick to your values, but your position requires stewardship and oversight of an organization with its own value set. You owe it to the district and the community to ensure its longevity. Activism occurs when a single issue or value you hold supersedes all others, regardless of the district's values or student outcomes. Well-meaning community members often run on a single issue, get elected, then persist in that activist mentality as board members—forcing their values on the district without regard for student outcomes. Aside from the fact that these rarely concern student outcomes, the bigger issue is that this becomes a paradigm that the board members use to color all their other votes and interactions.

They may not want to vote to approve funds for after-school tutoring because the social issue they care about remains underfunded. So, this becomes a battle over dollars rather than a group of adults working in the best interest of students.

Often, this happens when groups push their values onto specific board members or candidates. Sometimes the candidates come from the community group pushing the contrasting values. You can look back at the previous section on value interplay to see how focusing purely on group values can lead to this role of activism from an elected position.

Trying to govern from an activist mindset undermines your ability to succeed in board governance. As someone elected to govern, you need to bear in mind the success of the entire district. Focusing on the district's success includes each kid, parent, and taxpayer. I'm not naive enough to think you can make decisions that are going to make each person happy. Utopias don't exist. However, you could make policies and decisions that favor one group of students over another.

The role of governance is vital to ensuring long-term success, which aligns with our definition and the stewardship of resources. When I was our board president, a group of community members was causing a stir in our district. I went and spoke at one of their meetings. Despite their positive intentions, what they requested was against state law. So, I asked them at the very beginning, "Who would rather see their taxpayer dollars go to fund teacher salaries and help students improve their academics rather than fighting lawsuits?" Every hand went up, including mine.

I agreed with the fight they were engaging in. I wanted the same things they did, but I had to take a stand against their group values, step out of the role of activist, and engage as a steward governing the district and its resources.

Decentralization

Recognizing and defining these values is good, but it's insufficient. These values need to be put into practice for them to matter. You could spend an entire weekend writing these values down, but the work is fruitless unless they make it out of your notebook and into the organization's DNA.

One way for your values to make a difference is through decentralization. This process is done through the Decision Lens Matrix discussed later in the book. For now, I'll explain what decentralization is and why it matters in the context of school boards.

Understanding Decentralization

Centralization occurs when the district office makes a decision and informs everyone else of the policy. It's a bit dictatorial, and although this definition might seem harsh, there's a time and place for it. When I first joined my district board, I met with many members of the executive leadership team. I learned from our communications director about our schools' desire to centralize communication efforts. Centralizing communication was something the district wanted, too, to ensure consistent messaging across all our buildings.

Decentralization occurs when different departments or buildings are empowered to make decisions independently. Effectively, the leader closest to the issue makes the decisions. This method requires holding things a little looser, but more importantly, it requires trust and guidelines. Teams without trust or with low trust won't have the same latitude or the flexibility to address issues on their own, which breeds frustration. Without careful consideration, it can turn into a haves-and-have-nots situation.

Security is a great thing to centralize. Everyone is doing the same thing in the same way. The security team can operate as needed, and everyone knows what to expect, regardless of which location they're visiting. It would be a nightmare for your security team to allow five different buildings to handle their protocols differently. In this instance, centralization isn't a bad thing—it's necessary. However, this is simply one side of the decision equation.

Given the security topic, evacuation plans would be a better candidate for decentralization. Ensuring an evacuation plan exists is part of the district's (centralized) overarching security protocol. Still, the specifics of the plan and the procedures for evacuating a building should be decentralized. Not only are buildings designed differently, requiring some flexibility to navigate, but the property and terrain are different, too. Each building has different surroundings, so where everyone goes once they leave a door depends on which building they're in. In addition, if you're evacuating due to a specific threat, such as a fire, the leader must assess the threat's location to develop the best evacuation plan to protect the staff and students in their care. One-size-fits-all evacuation plans would be impractical.

As you can see, there's a place for both centralization and decentralization. The problem many new leaders face is how to implement decentralization guardrails appropriately. Decentralization provides flexibility, while centralization ensures efficiency through standardization—leaders must balance both. It's a delicate balance; you must pick one to lean on. But knowing your own values, as well as those of the board and district, will go a long way toward implementing these guardrails.

I'll close out the work around values for now. As this book is about Values-Based Governance, I assure you it will be an ongoing theme. This chapter is just foundational work regarding values. Now we will move on to our last building block before diving into the complete VBG framework.

Homework – Chapter 3

1. What are some of the core values that have guided your decision-making in the past? How have these values been shaped by your upbringing, experiences, and beliefs?

2. Reflecting on a recent decision, how did your values influence that decision? How might the decision have been different if you prioritized different values?

3. Imagine you are on a school board. What potential conflicts arise between your values, the board's, the district's, and societal/group values? How would you navigate those tensions when making decisions?

4. Describe when you felt pressure from a group or organization to compromise your values. How did you handle that situation, and what insights did you gain about staying true to your principles?

5. What concrete steps can you take to understand and articulate your core values better? How might defining your values more clearly help you be a more effective leader or decision-maker in your community?

Chapter 4:
Leadership Challenges

Chapter Summary:

In this chapter, you'll understand the unique challenges facing school boards, from operating in the public sector to serving involuntary families. You'll learn about supply-and-demand issues in board leadership, organizational drift, and why strong values-based leaders are essential. By the end, you'll know how to build trust with all stakeholders and avoid common leadership pitfalls.

Now we must complete our foundational work before diving into the nuts and bolts of the Values-Based Governance framework. One of the core concepts in principle-based policy work is to focus on the "why" first and let the "how" follow naturally. With this in mind, I will explain the "why" of Values-Based Governance now, so we can more effectively understand the "how" when we get there. Looking at the why is where the final part of our definition comes in:

...aiming for ethical and effective management.

Over the past decade, I've spoken with many new school board members from urban, rural, and suburban areas. The primary, consistent theme I've heard is, "I had no idea what I was getting into." This uncertainty is unfortunate because it leads to frustration stemming from unmet expectations. As frustration increases, the likelihood of someone remaining on a school board for their whole term decreases.

These unmet expectations can happen for several reasons. The actual reasons don't matter as much as the fact that it's happening, and it's happening often. The resulting frustration leads to a shortage of individuals willing to serve on a school board.

I previously provided an entire chapter on governance, so we won't revisit all of those factors here. However, I do want to discuss the uniqueness of serving on a school board and the challenges facing our community. Again, I'm trying to explain why this book's framework matters and define the problem it solves. School boards are unique, and I want to ensure new members have appropriate expectations to reduce friction and maintain a steady supply of strong, effective leaders.

Operating in the Public Sector

Boards of education exist in the public sector. School districts are governmental entities because taxpayer dollars primarily fund them. Being a public entity provides its share of challenges and opportunities. Let's take a look at some of those below.

Transparency. Transparency has become a significant factor in the public sector, both operationally and financially. Because tax dollars fund public entities, the community deserves to know how much the district spends and how it spends those funds each year. Because of this requirement for financial transparency, every district provides its community with the budget and an accounting of expenses. In many cases, state law requires annual audits to ensure proper financial controls are in place. Operational transparency allows the community to view meetings, view records of board votes, and access policies. The pursuit of transparency doesn't give the public a license to interrupt meetings or make demands; however, it does require the district to provide processes and opportunities for taxpayers to access this information.

Funding. School districts and all other public entities rely on taxes as their primary funding source. These taxes are paid to the district whether or not you have students in the school system. This results in a relatively static, predictable funding model year over year. The persistent and consistent nature of this funding gives some public entities the latitude to shirk their financial responsibility, as they don't have to put forth much effort to cover next year's budget. Because everyone in the district pays taxes, you inevitably end up with people who are unhappy with how the district uses their tax dollars. Such consternation is understandable and directly ties back to the need for financial transparency as mentioned above.

Accountability. One unique aspect of the public sector is that there are often no alternatives. For our purposes, you pay into a single school district, whether it meets your needs or not. If your district fails or you don't have children, you still fund your local schools. Even if you participate in alternative options, like private schools, the district still collects your tax dollars for the schools in your neighborhood. This captive funding model puts a whole new focus on accountability. The superintendent is accountable to the board of education, who are held accountable by the community. As your financers (read: taxpayers) are involuntary, proper checks and balances are key. The concept of involuntary patrons is another aspect of transparency that I will discuss in greater detail later in this chapter.

« »

With that context in place, it's crucial to discuss leadership issues in the public sector, specifically in public education, and how the Values-Based Governance framework addresses them.

Over the past decade, I've seen the need for strong leaders to govern school boards. Two of the most significant errors I've witnessed are board members betraying their personal beliefs and values under external pressure from groups, and abdicating governance-level duties to the administration team. These blunders shouldn't be a surprise, as I've already covered them both in previous chapters.

Supply and Demand

Every county and state has school boards. In some counties, like where I served, there are even more. We had over 12 districts and nearly 20 charter schools in our county alone. When you figure that each board has, on average, five members, that results in over 150 distinct people needed to fill every board seat in one county in one state, which has more than 60 counties, and those are just public, K-12 school boards. That number doesn't include private schools or state-level boards.

As you can see, there is a considerable need in each community for good leaders to step up and make a differ-

Leadership Challenges

ence. I have served on three public boards: two school boards and our local library district. I served as both a regular board member and the board president of each board. I understand the time commitment. I know firsthand how it takes away from my family and work. I've missed my kid's soccer games and school events because of board obligations. It didn't happen often, but it happened. This reality has kept many Americans focused on their families and careers rather than on civic service.

These factors have created a significant gap between supply and demand.

I've seen school board vacancies where no applications were received, leaving the seat unfilled and the board shorthanded. The lack of supply leads the board to settle for the willing rather than the qualified; however, the willing might not be there to serve the district's or students' best interests. I've seen plenty of people elected to local school boards who focus more on political games than on student achievement. And this is a persistent part of the problem. There are highly dedicated individuals who do not concentrate on improving their boards or districts. Our students are stuck with political agents because the leaders they deserve aren't willing to step up and serve their community.

Part of the reason for writing this book is to inform the average citizen that school board seats are accessible. I want to build the supply pool so more people can help carry the load. Getting involved with your student's school and local district will help you become familiar with their operations and needs. By attending your local school board meetings (or simply watching online), you'll get a sense of the issues facing the district, the district's academic and curricular status, and why it's crucial to have strong leaders on the board. You can start moving up the learning curve now, because we don't need just anyone to fill these board seats, as this has been the current methodology in many districts nationwide. We need the right people to fill these seats.

Strong Leadership

The right people for school boards are strong leaders. Our communities need people who can align the district's mission and vision with their values to create action. To oversimplify and make my point, I'm defining three types of leaders: The Well-Meaning Do-Nothing, The Narcissistic Tyrant, and The Values-Based Leader. The first two types are the most prevalent on boards because people either want to give back altruistically or have an agenda to push through.

Before I explain these three types of board members, I want to be clear. Just having good values doesn't make you a values-based leader. I share my value system with many people in my community who couldn't lead a horse to water, let alone an entire organization. Thus, it's essential to understand why communities must look for people with strong values who are also good leaders.

The Well-Meaning Do-Nothing. These folks are wonderful people. They're easy to get along with because this is precisely what they want. They don't cause division. They don't cause problems. But they don't cause change, which is where the rub exists. The status quo is the path of least resistance. These members champion the status quo rather than pushing for significant change. Rubber-stamp boards, or "The Appeasers," are comprised of this type of person, as they don't tend to push back against the administration or other board members. These individuals focus more on the organization's goals than on any other value system.

The Narcissistic Tyrant. Many who decide to sit on a school board fall into this category. They believe they're the ones standing between salvation and assured destruction. A hero complex, if you will. Often, they come in with an agenda and a change plan, eschewing all who stand in their way. The main issue I've seen with these board members is their Machiavellian tendencies, which erode trust among board members, administration, staff, and the community. These individuals tend to focus more on either their own values or group values than anything else. The Stair-Stepper, The Crusader, and The Hand-on Hero are all versions of The Narcissistic Tyrant leadership type.

The Values-Based Leader. These individuals can make effective changes within an organization. They're on the board to partner with the organization and improve it. These leaders focus on aligning values, outcomes, and actions, which results in the district running more efficiently. The value-based leader balances their values with those of the district, the board, and the community to support effective governance and student success.

I've witnessed these values-based leaders make significant changes. They've brought order to budgets, pushed for strategic messaging, increased academic outcomes, and given the organization a better reputation in the community. They build relationships with the administration and other community leaders or board members across geographic areas. Values-based leadership is good governance.

The words and depictions listed above may seem biased. They are, but I started by saying this was an intentional oversimplification. And let's be honest, nobody wants to be the first two types of board members, so you're more inclined to self-identify as the latter and work to resolve the cognitive dissonance between your past actions and the description of the values-based leader throughout the rest of this book.

Organizational Drift

Unfortunately, organizational drift has made many organizations anemic. They spend money on initiatives that don't advance their mission, which is in direct contrast to strategic alignment as a concept. It's a tendency many districts, and even businesses, have to fight against. Often, districts use surveys and forums to solicit community feedback on programming or services that would be beneficial. The district will then work to fill the void as these seem like good ideas. Just because good ideas exist doesn't mean they align with the mission. Engaging in these "other projects" is where organizational drift is most evident.

Mission creep is one element of organizational drift. One of the most flagrant examples I've seen stemmed from a bill passed by the Colorado State House of Representatives in 2020. The bill required school districts to have school counselors or social workers at each grade level. In many cases, this would require a school to hire five additional counselors, costing districts around $300,000 per elementary school annually.

This bill initiated a pilot program, and one of its stated goals was to reduce the district's parents' unemployment rate. Although this is a laudable effort, it's not the core purpose of a school district. The district's mission is to educate and prepare students for life after high school, not to increase the employment rates of adults.

As concerning as mission creep is, there's more to organizational drift. Another aspect is societal drift. This drift comes from societal values moving over time. Societal values tend to shift like pendulums, meaning that as they move further in one direction, it's only a matter of time before they swing back the other way. These changes can be problematic as the board would make long-term changes for short-term reasons.

As an example, when working with one board, there was a non-discrimination policy listing many different groups that the district wouldn't discriminate against. Although it was a well-intentioned policy, the wording required it to evolve as societal norms shifted. As new groups and classes gained "protected" status, the district regularly updated the policy to ensure it included each group. The board took a simple approach, stating they wouldn't discriminate against anyone. The policy doesn't bend to societal shifts, yet it still serves its intended purpose of codifying the district's non-discrimination stance.

Student success and academic outcomes span these societal shifts.

Involuntary Families

One facet of education that makes board work different is the distinction between voluntary and involuntary patrons. When I served on the charter school board, every family had chosen to attend our school. There were no boundaries, neighborhoods, or busing, just families committed to our vision, mission, and pedagogy (educational philosophy and methodology for educating students).

It was refreshing because when people didn't like what was happening at the school, they would find another school to serve their students' needs. We existed as an option and accepted as many families as possible each year.

However, when you serve on a district's board of education, it's imperative to understand that the families in your district are *involuntary* clients. Regardless of a family's choices, the district must serve that family's needs. The buck stops with you, and the family knows the district is responsible for serving them.

So, this becomes a delicate balancing act in leadership when a group of voters elects you to your position. Still, you represent every family in the district, the ones who voted for you and those who didn't, those who like you, and those who post hand-drawn cartoons on social media or print slanderous fliers about you (all actual examples, by the way).

You represent them all, and your decisions affect them all. You have to internalize the uniqueness of working for people who don't want to be in your district and acknowledge that you must ensure the success of every student, including theirs.

I've seen new board members act like politicians, which can lead them to focus on the values of your community and the groups working to get you elected, neglecting your own or those of the district. Suppose you win an election with a ten-point margin, 55% to 45%, which is a good margin. I've heard new board members say this is a mandate from their community to push their values and force district conformity to their values (or a group's values).

But what if voter turnout was only 30% of your district? That turns your 55% into 16.5% of the community. Now, you're trying to explain that you represent the majority of voters in the district, even though you received votes from less than 17% of the community. It's a dangerous precedent to make sweeping decisions for the entire district when you pretend 17% is close to 80%. Behaving this way will quickly isolate families.

In an effort to work with your involuntary clients and show them you care about their needs and ensure the success of their students, here are three strategies for engaging the involuntary clients in your district.

Build trust. Involuntary families may be skeptical of district motives or resistant to decisions made by the board. To counteract this, being as transparent as possible about decision-making processes, budgeting, and policy changes is crucial. Communicate early and often, but also strategically. Don't mistake strategic communication for a lack of transparency. You also want to ensure your communication is consistent with all stakeholders, not just those who support you. Be authentic and humble. Be quick to help, be a leader, and focus on the things discussed in the governance chapter—no need to rehash all of that here.

Focus on shared values. While involuntary families may disagree with specific policies or decisions, most share a common desire for quality education and student success. Build on these commonalities to unite all stakeholders. When engaging in policy discourse (or strategic communication), frame those discussions and decisions around these shared values. When conflict arises, try to base those conversations on how it will positively impact student outcomes. This approach can help bridge divides and remind everyone of the district's core mission.

Listen to all stakeholders. Getting feedback is critical to building trust with involuntary families, especially from groups that may feel underrepresented within the district. The feedback circuit could involve creating advisory committees that reflect the district's demographic makeup, conducting surveys to gather feedback on major decisions, or holding "linkages" or town halls in different parts of the district. Now, collecting the data doesn't mean you have to act on the feedback, but ensuring you listen to each group matters. Take the information, process it, and compare it to your mission, vision, outcomes, and values. One refrain you'll hear is that you're not listening to your constituents when you don't do what they say. That is 100% a false premise. I've stated on more than one occasion that I might draw different conclusions after analyzing the presented information, but that doesn't mean I didn't listen.

By implementing these strategies, board members can work more effectively with involuntary families, build a sense of community, and develop a shared purpose with stakeholders across the district—even among those who might not have chosen to be part of the district or feel trapped where they are. Remember, the goal is not to win every argument or please everyone, but to create an educational environment where all students can learn, regardless of their families' stance towards the district.

« »

When working with involuntary clients, you must build trust, focus on shared values, and listen to all stakeholders. Remember that not all students and families are involuntary, but many are. Focusing on these strategies will help you build rapport with the district, the teachers, and the broader community. Meetings and initiatives go much better when you can show you're on the board to help make the district better.

Serving on a district board requires a delicate balance of leadership, empathy, and strategic thinking. By acknowledging the involuntary nature of many families' relationships and actively addressing their concerns, board members can more effectively fulfill their responsibilities to all students and families in the district.

Homework – Chapter 4

1. Think about a recent decision made by your local school board. How did it balance the needs of voluntary and involuntary families in the district? How could the board have better served both groups?

2. Identify a potential example of "mission creep" or "organizational drift" in your local school district. How would you address this issue using the principles of Values-Based Governance?

3. Design a brief strategy to build trust with involuntary families in your district. Include specific actions you would take as a board member to implement this strategy.

4. Consider a controversial issue currently facing your local school district. How would you apply the principles of focusing on shared values and listening to all stakeholders to address this issue?

Part II:
The Model

Now that we've laid the foundation, Part II will describe the Values-Based Governance framework. We'll discuss the three facets of VBG, how they work together, and their role in effective governance. The upcoming chapters will discuss higher-level strategies rather than tactics. The goal is for you to understand the model and start relating the core tenets of Values-Based Governance to your district, experience, and governance style. All districts are different and need to apply the framework contextually. Therefore, nothing that follows is prescriptive, but it provides you with a model for successful governance.

As we get into the meat of the framework, it's important to remember the homework sections in each chapter. Some of the content may seem daunting or complicated to assimilate into a cohesive approach for your district. When that happens, read through the homework questions—they'll help you understand how to start making the necessary connections. These exercises are essential to your overall understanding of the framework.

5 five

Chapter 5:
Values-Based Governance

Chapter Summary:

In this chapter, you'll learn the complete VBG framework and its three core tenets: Strategic Alignment, Policy Development, and Cultural Adaptation. You'll see how these tenets work together to create sustainable change and how they relate to sound governance principles. By the end, you'll understand the complete VBG model and be ready to dive further into implementing it in your district.

Since we've completed the foundational building blocks of Values-Based Governance (VBG), we can start working through the actual framework—what it is and how to use it. First, you need to understand that VBG is a governance system, not a policy model. Being a framework means it aligns with your board's current methodology for handling policy, which is an advantage because it doesn't require you to make any shifts in implementing your policy book. You can adopt VBG on your own and start to see the benefits in your district.

Just as with any framework, VBG simply provides a structure. How you use it determines its effectiveness. VBG will help you build relationships quickly, both laterally and vertically, which is crucial when you're an outsider joining the board. No one in the organization knows who you are, what you believe, or how you approach things. I've experienced this firsthand, including leaders lying about me and my reputation to their staff, putting me at odds before I had a single conversation or sat through my first board meeting.

Because I practice Values-Based Governance, I've successfully served with people from every corner of the political spectrum. Since we've worked together closely, they have continually come to my defense. I've earned a reputation for making organizations better by partnering with them to advance their missions rather than imposing my own. It's not about changing *what* the district does, but rather about *how* the district accomplishes its mission, ensuring it operates in a principle-based way.

Every new board member is an outsider, and all too often, I see them try to prove how smart and accomplished they are. Newly seated members will try to show how their ideas will save the district, but because they're coming in as outsiders and unknowns, nobody in the administration cares what they have to say. When you're an outsider, you must prove you want to be a team player and care about the district before your thoughts or words mean anything. You demonstrate this "team-player" attitude through relationship-building and spending time with the organization's leadership. Your values don't mean anything until you've earned the right and permission to speak into the organization. Enter Values-Based Governance.

Core Tenets

Values-Based Governance has three central tenets: strategic alignment, policy development, and cultural adaptation. I'll discuss these tenets in greater detail in the upcoming chapters, but first, I want to provide an overview of the concepts here and how they complement each other to enhance your district's effectiveness.

Strategic Alignment

Strategic alignment occurs when your operations and day-to-day actions align with your mission, vision, and core values. Although this sounds easy, it can be quite a messy knot to untangle, especially when you're dealing with a governmental organization that has existed for decades.

Using VBG as a framework can bring renewed focus and efficiency to your organization, reducing operating costs, increasing staff morale, and strengthening stakeholder support. These benefits result from being intentional with your time and efforts as a board and from setting expectations and accountability measures for your superintendent and their administrative team.

In the next chapter, we'll discuss how difficult it can be to stay focused on your organization's mission and vision. You have to be able to define and clearly express what you want as an outcome, align your district's operations to that specific outcome, and then pursue it relentlessly.

Strategically aligning your district doesn't mean there won't be distractions along the way. Any board member in their role for more than four months has sat through their share of minutiae, legal briefs, and other off-mission topics. So, despite your best efforts as a board member to stay focused solely on your mission and vision, you will always spend time on other matters.

However, as a board, you must demonstrate determination to push through and focus as much time as possible on your defined outcomes, which should be student success as a school district.

Policy Development

As the second core tenet, policy development is crucial to maintaining strategic alignment. As a board member, you ensure the district's policies reflect the mission and vision. If something doesn't exist in policy, you can't hold anyone accountable because there aren't clear expectations. Without policy, expectations are only myths.

Staff look to policy for two primary reasons. The first reason is to know what to do in certain situations. From the top down, everyone in your organization deserves clarity regarding expectations. Policy helps create clarity. Good policy should be objective and yield consistent interpretations among everyone who reads it. As previously stated, frustration stems from unmet expectations. Defining your expectations explicitly ensures everyone understands them—a necessary precursor to meeting them. Clear expectations also increase policy adherence.

Staff members also utilize policy as a reference point to balance their own professional judgment with established organizational guidelines. This process ensures that individual actions align with broader institutional goals and legal requirements, while also providing a framework for accountability.

As board members, you must be committed to well-crafted policy. Knowing the significant role policy plays in guiding staff actions and ensuring organizational alignment, it is essential to embrace the responsibility of developing it thoughtfully and thoroughly. This commitment should drive us to lean into the process and make policy the best it can be. The policies your board creates will be a critical resource for many staff members, and they deserve well-crafted policies. We'll cover the actual policy creation in Chapter 7.

Cultural Adaptation

The final tenet of Values-Based Governance is cultural adaptation, from an organizational perspective. Even though you work to strategically align your mission, vision, and core values with your desired outcomes and create policy to support those outcomes, you won't necessarily get where you want to go. The people in your organization are the ones who put all of this into practice. You will never reach your desired destination without the staff, volunteers, and leadership working together. The culture of the organization matters.

When discussing governance previously, I mentioned how important trust is. Cultural adaptation is why trust is crucial to good governance. You can't implement policy without your staff. Employees carry the cultural torch and do the hard work every day, but if the administration doesn't trust you, they won't hold employees accountable for following policy. Your policies and mission will merely exist as words on paper, and accountability becomes impossible.

Culture requires trust, however that alone isn't enough. When implementing Values-Based Governance, culture must also include accountability and confidence—the 'Holy Trinity' of culture: trust, accountability, and confidence. Together, these three create the foundation for successful VBG implementation. I know all of this sounds like something "easier said than done," which it is, but there is a path forward. I will discuss the implementation side of culture in Chapter 8. You won't be left alone.

Bringing the Framework Together

Let me put it simply: Strategic alignment defines your values. Policy development embeds your values in the district. Cultural adaptation implements those values daily.

As a leader, it's your responsibility to cast a vision, set the course, and sail towards the horizon. You'll need to spot-check periodically to ensure you're still on the right path to reach your end goal, but the vision should not change or waver. Ensuring you have the proper vision cast and in focus is part of the strategic alignment process.

Once your organization's vision is in place, you will need to create a policy that describes what that vision looks like in your organization and how it will be implemented, thereby aligning vision and operations. The board shouldn't focus on day-to-day tasks, as this is the administration's domain. Policy is how you connect the board's vision with district operations, achieve strategic alignment, and ultimately hold your administration accountable for policy adherence. Having the board's vision codified in policy will make it easy for everyone in the organization to see, comprehend, and execute.

Once the board creates policy, the process shifts to cultural adaptation, ensuring the administration implements the vision with fidelity. District culture must support the work you're doing as a board. Your staff must have buy-in as they implement the board's vision. The administrative team and building-level staff are the arbiters and do the actual hard work required to meet the board's vision.

Relating VBG to Good Governance

After reviewing the aforementioned tenets of Values-Based Governance, let's quickly compare them to our descriptors of good governance, which, as a reminder, are accountability, teamwork, and leadership.

Values-Based Governance

Strategic alignment is aligning your mission, vision, and values. To reach such alignment, the board must first define the organization's mission, vision, and values. Casting a vision is an essential aspect of leadership. Decision-making becomes easier once the vision, mission, and values are in place. Doing the right thing is much simpler when you already have a predetermined frame of reference. Your mission and vision will serve as that frame of reference, your North Star. From a leadership perspective, it's incumbent upon you to make decisions that reflect the organization's defined values, as outlined in the mission and vision.

Policy development is the accountability piece of Values-Based Governance. Without a clear, well-defined policy, there is no accountability. Determining your mission, casting a vision, and distilling it into applicable written instructions is nearly an art form. Because this work has far-reaching implications for accountability, you should take the effort seriously. The policies created must be coherent and digestible by everyone in your organization.

Policy is only one part of accountability, as policy adherence is binary, meaning it's either followed or not. More work is required to ensure your mission and vision are actively advanced. For such forward progress to occur, work must continue constantly. Your board must set goals and benchmarks to hold your administration accountable for that movement, which rounds out the accountability aspect of good governance.

Teamwork is the final piece to good governance, and it's where cultural adaptation takes flight. As previously stated, the board doesn't have the time or capacity to implement the district's mission and vision. Instead, they set guidance and expectations through policy, but the board must rely on district staff to carry out this work. That's teamwork.

Like in any team sport, each player has a role and must rely on their teammates to perform their tasks. Your organization is a team of smaller teams, each composed of people. Since no single team can accomplish the district's mission, each team must trust the others to do their part in advancing the district's mission and vision.

The interplay between the Values-Based Governance tenets hints at the complicated nature of leading an organization. Despite the complexity of this framework, there's a practical way to begin. You have to start by knowing where you want to go, which is the organization's mission, vision, and values. Objectively identifying where you are is step one, which informs direction and guides the careful, intentional development of policy. The developed policies, mission, and vision provide a framework for accountability. During all of this, it's vital to build relationships and establish trust with the people in the organization.

Resolving Against the Definition

Let's revisit the definition of Values-Based Governance from Chapter 1. VBG is:

> an approach to leading and stewarding an organization where decisions and actions are guided by a set of core values, aligning personal, organizational, and stakeholder principles and aiming for ethical and effective management.

Now, let's break this down and reference back to the core tenets of VBG.

Leading and stewarding an organization speaks to both strategic alignment and policy. To lead an organization, you must cast the vision and set the course. Strategic alignment and policy drive stewardship: strategic alignment sets stewardship as a value, and policies ensure the organization executes stewardship throughout.

Values-Based Governance

Decisions and actions are guided by a set of core values, which again speaks to strategic alignment and policy, but this also goes into culture. The strategic alignment process creates a set of core values. Those core values guide and inform policy creation, which the district translates into decisions and actions. Culture will then adapt to the district's core values to ensure actions and decisions are consistent with policy, which the district achieves through accountability processes.

Aligning personal, organizational, and stakeholder principles for ethical and effective management starts with strategic alignment, in which diverse values converge into a single theme. Effective management requires clear accountability and appropriate policies. Cultural adaptation helps ensure ethics and effectiveness are priorities throughout the organization.

As you can see, the definition of Values-Based Governance reflects the core tenets. As these tenets align with good governance, the simplicity of this framework masks the complex interweaving required to create effective governance. In the following chapters, we'll explore the specific *what's* and *how's* of each tenet within the Values-Based Governance framework to utilize the model for effective governance.

Homework – Chapter 5

1. Reflect on your organization's current mission and vision statements. How well do they align with the day-to-day operations? Identify one area where you could improve strategic alignment.

2. Think of a recent policy decision made by your board. How did it reflect (or not reflect) your organization's core values? What would you change to align it with the tenets of Values-Based Governance?

3. Describe a situation where your organization's culture conflicted with its stated values or policies. How would you use cultural adaptation to address this disconnect?

4. As a new or potential board member, outline a strategy to build trust and relationships within your organization while staying true to your values. How would this strategy help you implement Values-Based Governance effectively?

5. Choose one upcoming decision your board needs to make. Apply the Values-Based Governance framework to this decision, considering strategic alignment, policy development, and cultural adaptation. How does this approach change your perspective on the decision?

Chapter 6:
Strategic Alignment

Chapter Summary:

In this chapter, you'll learn how to align your district's mission, vision, and values with daily operations and outcomes. You'll see practical examples of staying focused on student achievement and avoiding mission drift. By the end, you'll know how to create strategic alignment that keeps everyone focused on what matters most: student success.

As discussed in the previous chapter, the first tenet of Values-Based Governance is strategic alignment: defining your mission, vision, values, and related documents, which we'll refer to as the foundational documents. The first step is to create a unified mission, vision, and core value set for your district. Your organization should already have some set of these statements defined, which will be a great starting point. You should continually evaluate them to see if they still represent you, your board, and your district appropriately.

You should first look at your district's desired outcomes: the organization's end goal. This goal should be defined in simple terms, so everyone can understand it and discuss it. Once the board states the outcomes, focus the mission and vision on them. If the mission and vision don't point to your desired outcomes, they need to change.

Core values are harder to define because your board members may have differing or conflicting values. Regardless of how far apart your board might seem here, it's essential to go through the process to find common ground. At some level, you'll find values similar enough to focus on, like academic success for all students.

In the context of a school board, the mission is simple: to educate students. You'd think that in a school district it would be easy to implement strategic alignment throughout the organization, but then you'd be wrong. I've worked with plenty of districts and witnessed enough board meetings to know that simple and easy are rarities in school districts. Too many board members are grandstanding in front of their communities to boost their self-importance. Humility is a lost virtue.

In addition, it can be rather easy to get distracted by shiny fads, which will cause you to stray off course and down the path of mission drift. And what makes this difficult is that these educational crazes are not all bad things; some of these efforts are good things to do for your

Strategic Alignment

students or community, even though they take you off mission. However, just because they're good doesn't mean you should change your mission to provide these services. Let me give you an example.

As a school district, we serve many kids. These kids come from different backgrounds, creeds, and socioeconomic statuses. We have kids with single parents working two and three jobs to make ends meet, and we have students from dual-income families, each parent making six figures. Those are diverse populations for a single team to oversee, each with widely varying needs. Students perform better when fed a nutritious breakfast and a healthy lunch. Kids with enough sleep attend school with their minds rested and ready to learn.

Because your mission is to educate kids, they should be in the best mental, physical, and emotional state to learn. So, should your district serve breakfast to students? Should you ensure all students have a roof over their heads and a bed to sleep on? Is it the school district's responsibility to help parents find jobs so they can better care for and provide for the students you're responsible for educating?

These are all good things. Kids need stability. Their mental and emotional well-being is tied closely to physiological needs, which are the first two steps in Maslow's Hierarchy of Needs. But should the district be responsible for providing these services? Not at all. It's not the school district's job to care for those underlying needs. Parents and families need to take responsibility here. When the district starts spending resources on food and shelter for students, it's taking dollars away from teachers, classroom materials, curriculum, and other items needed for a successful education. You can spend significant, valuable resources on off-mission projects simply because they're good ideas. As a board member, you must be vigilant to ensure your district stays focused on your mission.

Written Reports for Board Meetings

If you'll remember back in the "Values-Based Governance in Practice" section, I told you how I cleaned up our agendas and reduced our meeting time by nearly 60%. This section references one strategy I used to shorten meetings. The whole revision process is in Chapter 8.

When I was president of my school board, I stopped allowing presentations during board meetings when they didn't directly impact student outcomes. As board members, we were responsible for modeling the desired attitude and culture in our school buildings. If I wanted everyone to focus their time and attention on student outcomes and academic success, I would model a relentless focus on academics in the boardroom.

We still had many items requiring attention, but we didn't spend much time on them. Other presenters would submit their packets as written reports for our board to review before the meeting, while I omitted other items from our agenda altogether. Because these written reports were part of our board packet, all relevant materials were available to the public for review before our board meeting. If any member had questions, concerns, or comments about the written reports, they were welcome to raise them. Staff would then be available to answer questions, so the board could adequately perform its due diligence on that specific agenda item. But we only discussed those written reports as needed. When presentations were required for the board to vote on something, I added time limits to keep the presenter focused and on track.

However, the board generously allowed time to discuss test scores, graduation requirements, academic results, and career education. That's why we were there: to focus on helping students successfully graduate and launch into their post-K-12 careers.

Resolving the disconnect between our meetings and our mission was the first step our board took to ensure our mission, vision, and values aligned with our behavior. Our boardroom became the place to model strategic alignment and focus our time and attention on the organization's mission. Believe it or not, this was a significant shift for our district's board. I'd been to meetings throughout the years, even before sitting on the board, and I watched presentations on many topics that weren't advancing our district's student growth or achievement. Although it was a substantial deviation from the norm, it was well-received by our board and leadership team.

Our board also had a new superintendent who focused on foundational teaching skills. She designed this initiative to get our administrators and building leaders on the same page and bring pedagogical consistency across the district. The goal was to ensure that the district developed a strong curriculum for every grade level, that staff created and administered common assessments, and that all teachers used similar classroom methodologies.

To kick off this effort, our superintendent conducted a district-wide book study involving over 150 teachers and administrators. When the study began, the superintendent invited our board to join, and most of us accepted her offer. Participating in a district-wide book study was another way for the board to model aligning our time with the district's mission of educating children. Not only could we lead by example, but many of the district leaders appreciated that our board took an interest in their work. It helped us build relationships by sitting down to discuss the best instructional standards and how we could support the teams working in each school.

« »

Strategic alignment is a top-down practice. You have to start broad and then narrow it down. The board, encompassing the entire district, must be the broad starting point. The superintendent and the administration are then held accountable to the same standard. Once the board, superintendent, and executive leadership team are strategically aligned, it's time to narrow the focus to the principals, deans, department chairs, or team leads, and classroom teachers. You can see how this process creates a pyramid shape, starting wide and broad and gradually narrowing into strategically aligned practice within each classroom. This process will take time, to be sure, but it's one of the most critical pieces to get right when you want to implement Values-Based Governance.

Remember, the district's mission, vision, and core values are examples of Organizational Values. It's not your job to go in and change all those foundational documents to align with your values. Your job initially is to ensure the mission, vision, and values are narrow enough to be acted upon well. Once the board defines the foundational documents in a way that allows you to work towards them, you must ensure everyone focuses on the desired outcomes.

Don't worry. I layout the process for creating these documents in Chapter 9.

Homework – Chapter 6

1. Review your district's current mission and vision statements. How well do they align with your desired student outcomes? Propose one specific change that would improve this alignment.

2. Identify one "off-mission" activity or program in your district that, while beneficial, may be diverting resources from core educational goals. How would you approach evaluating and addressing this misalignment using Values-Based Governance principles?

3. Reflect on your board's meeting structure. What percentage of time does the board spend on items directly related to student outcomes? Outline a plan to refocus board meetings on mission-critical topics, similar to the example in the chapter.

4. Consider a recent district-wide initiative. As a board member, how could you actively participate in and model strategic alignment for this initiative? Describe specific actions you would take to demonstrate your commitment and encourage others to follow suit.

seven
7

Chapter 7:
Policy Development

Chapter Summary:

In this chapter, you'll understand the critical role of policy in embedding values throughout your organization. You'll learn the difference between operational and governing policies, see examples of good versus bad policy, and explore different governance models. By the end, you'll know how to create values-based policies that guide decision-making at every level.

Policy is where you embed values within the organization, which is the natural next step after developing your mission, vision, and core values. Values can't be embedded if they aren't defined. Despite many board members rolling their eyes at the thought, policy development is the hard, critical work of any governing board. Policy is too often "set it and forget it" in organizations, meaning once the board develops and deploys a policy, they rarely review it.

In many governance models, the board reviews its policies on a regular, biannual review calendar, but the frequency can vary depending on the policy model. Despite this regular audit, many boards only "review" the policies and move on. There is too much jargon or rote legal vernacular to make the language accessible for your average board member, many of whom are regular folks trying to do a little good in their community.

The complexity doesn't excuse a lack of due diligence regarding policy review. I've seen 25-year-old policies without any recorded reviews or changes. Think about how much has changed in your community over three decades. You owe it to your constituency to ensure your policies are up to date and fully reflect your organization's values. And you must ask yourself, if no one has reviewed said policy, are you sure staff are following it?

Different Types of Policy

There are two main types of policies. You'll see different terms used depending on which policy and governance models your board uses, but I'll refer to them as operational and governing. You must understand the differences between these two types of policy, as districts don't always break them out correctly. This distinction, when wielded appropriately, gives both clarity and empowerment to employees.

I worked with a board that embedded governing policies into operational policies. It had been done this way for years, with the board reviewing one to two paragraphs on each policy. This format was problematic because of the sheer number of policies. After advocating for a shift in how this organization considered and wrote policy, I learned that the board had hundreds of policies it had never reviewed (or even been aware of). These were all attached to employee-level policies outside the board's standard review process.

Before continuing, I need to mention the natural tension between the board and the administration. The board changes more often than the administration does. This turnover cycle causes some instability in leadership, as policy changes can be rapid and volatile when voters elect a new group to the governing board. Due to human nature and the need for stability and security, many administrators will try to diminish a board's impact on the organization, which isn't necessarily intentional or malicious on the part of the leadership. It is the natural progression in preserving the organization's stability over time.

This self-protection is likely what happened with the district mentioned above. Over time, the board relinquished more of its policy-making authority to the administration, to the point that the board's policies themselves were anemic and lacked impact. They were effectively belief statements, which weren't real policies at all. Recognizing this, I advocated for the board to take back ownership of their policy book, and thus began the process of recreating all board policies to ensure the board retained proper authority to govern the district.

Now, let's look at the different types of policies and how they work.

Operational

Operational policies indicate how the organization should function. These policies are procedures or protocols often created by the administrative team. Some examples of operational policies include how your buildings should look and feel, when reports are due, and hiring procedures.

An easy way to distinguish operational policies is to focus on "how" within the organization rather than the "why." These operational policies are directive, covering everything staff members need to know, including how to interact with other staff members and stakeholders in your district. The number of these policies can become rather voluminous, and I remember joking when I first started on the school board about how our operational policies would stand nearly six feet tall when stacked.

Organizational policies are the closest policies to your staff. As such, they should be written clearly and concisely and provide enough information for each employee to understand the expectations. Remember, those who work in your organization will look to policy to inform their decisions and actions, so organizational policy needs to be just prescriptive enough to manage behaviors and move toward the district's desired outcomes.

Governing

Governing policy is a higher-level abstraction than operational policy. From a practical standpoint, this means that few of your employees will need to read these policies. Your administration and leadership teams, on the other hand, must have a strong working knowledge of your governing policies, but they won't permeate the organization as operational policies do.

Good governing policy will be values-based, keeping you and your board focused on the "why" and letting your administration team develop the "how." The delineation above helps keep everyone focused in the right space. Your role on the board is one of leadership, setting the course for the entire organization. Casting the vision and leading the district becomes impossible when you and your board focus on *how* things get done.

Distinguishing the Two Types

Imagine being the captain of a ship. You've got to keep your crew happy, which includes getting to your destination without running out of resources. You'll have to stop and replenish fresh water, food, etc., before reaching your destination. Attaining your goal requires efficiency in navigation and knowledge of the landscape. As the captain, do you have time to steer the ship, explain how to properly chop vegetables for stew, inspect the cleanliness of the deck, and study the maps to chart a course to the next stop effectively?

Let's agree that micromanaging all those facets is neither possible nor remotely practical. If the captain is going to do his job well, he needs to study the maps, locate the ship relative to landmasses, and ensure safe navigation. Similarly, board members are focusing on the wrong areas when they spend time chopping potatoes and inspecting the decks. They're getting caught up in the minutiae and working on the operational side of the organization.

Remember, you need to focus on *values* and casting the vision for the district. If you're trying to force value changes in the district, you're missing an opportunity, and frankly, you're missing the point of leadership. Focus on imparting your values into the organization. Those values will gain momentum and become a current, pulling people along with you. Others will attempt to swim in a different direction, but it will become obvious who is resisting and who is embracing these shifts in values-based policy. With the cultural current picking up steam, you can focus purely on the values and vision rather than ensuring staff properly cut the potatoes. I know this example may seem silly and oversimplified, but I've seen too many board members focus on "potato chopping" instead of values-driven leadership.

Now you might think it's vital to have clean floors and proportionally cut potatoes to ensure your students are cared for appropriately. That's wonderful, and governing policy should handle those tasks rather than direct management. You could approach this differently: "Because we believe in excellence and agency, we'll focus on hiring experts in their field who know their professional standards and regulations."

In this example policy, we start by affirming the values the organization prioritizes. Then, we take those values and relate them to a desired result—one about hiring employees. With this one policy line, we no longer have to inspect floors or cut potatoes ourselves. We expect everyone hired into our district to understand what it takes to perform their job duties successfully. Small details become an exercise in accountability rather than execution.

Good Policy vs. Bad Policy

Policy development is crucial to good governance, but for policy to be effective, it has to be *good* policy. I say this because I've seen (and produced) my share of bad policies. One of the biggest pitfalls I've witnessed is a board that is completely value-aligned crafting policy without appropriate checks, which can lead to groupthink. One-party rule often leads to bad policy.

As I said earlier, this isn't a partisan framework, so "one party here " means like-minded. If no one is willing to push back and challenge your policy work, your policies can be tone-deaf and biased. You should find ways to push around the edges during your policy discussions and work sessions. Look for loopholes and gaps. Don't be afraid to

Policy Development

ask "what if" questions and throw some complicated and outrageous examples onto the table. I always ask people outside of my organization to provide feedback on policy changes. They don't have the same context, framing, or bias that I (and my colleagues) have. Subsequently, they'll ask different questions than I would.

No matter how benign you think a given policy is, it must stand the test of extremism. All organizations function in exceptions rather than rules; your policies must withstand those extreme limits and exceptional situations over time. Good policy takes time to create, test, and debate, but it's worth the effort.

Going back to my career in software, when developing new applications, we had dedicated testers. These testing jobs exist to break, or attempt to break, the application. Knowing what the code is supposed to do makes it easy to ensure you get the right outcome. But what happens when you put alphabetical text in a calculator application? What if I insert a command to manipulate the database where all the passwords are stored? Hackers thrive in these scenarios; they break software applications by exploiting boundaries beyond their intended use. They live in exceptional cases.

Policy development is very similar. You need to test all of the fringe cases and ways people could use, and to a greater extent, misuse that policy. As the policy creator, it's difficult for you to know the use case you're trying to solve, and you may end up putting yourself in a position to abuse the policy. You know the intended parameters the board set. It becomes imperative to have someone on your team (or an outside perspective) review the policy and try to break it.

You need a policy hacker.

Another facet of good policy is that it's non-reactionary. Good policy is proactive, but there are times your board will need to create policy due to changes in state law or specific situations in your district or community. However, just because you're "reacting" to changes around you doesn't mean you have to respond in a reactive way.

Again, good policy takes time. It's much better to get policy right than to rush it. Taking your time is especially important when policy touches on emotional issues. Suppose a staff member commits fraud. In that case, it's a good idea to create a policy to prevent future criminal activity, but rashly creating a policy at the board level to block this behavior will lead to poor policy. The better path forward is to pause, breathe, and formulate a plan. Investigate the related activities to understand how the staff member committed fraud. Is this a value-oriented or a procedural issue? Making these determinations will help inform your team on whether this should become operational or governing policy.

Taking time to examine the environment and existing policies closely can provide an opportunity to review other financial controls currently in place at your organization. Do you need to implement any new procedures for handling money? Once you better understand the complete picture of who, what, and how, you can create a non-reactionary policy that works much more effectively in the long run.

Types of Policy Models

There are many different types of policy models. Below, you'll find a few standard models with short descriptions. I'll introduce you to the model, followed by how each model implements accountability measures, and the relationship between the board and the executive officer/superintendent. As a reminder, Values-Based Governance is policy-model-agnostic, meaning you can use any of the options below with VBG.

Traditional Model

The Traditional Model, or the "working board" model, is one of the oldest and most common governance structures. Its policy philosophy is reactive, developing policies to address specific issues as they arise. The process for policy development typically involves board members identifying problems requiring attention, committees drafting policies, and the full board discussing and approving them. Key implementation details include board members often having specific operational roles, frequent hands-on involvement in day-to-day operations, and slower decision-making due to the committee structure.

Accountability Measures: In the Traditional Model, the board achieves accountability through detailed reporting from committees. Regular financial audits, performance evaluations of executive leadership, and annual board self-assessments are standard practices. This model's hands-on nature allows for close monitoring of operations, but it can sometimes blur the lines between Governance and management.

Board-Executive Relationship: This model often results in a close working relationship between the board and the executive officer, as board members are frequently involved in operational details. While this can foster strong communication and understanding, it may also create tension when roles and boundaries are unclear. The executive may sometimes feel micromanaged due to the board's hands-on approach.

Complementary Model

The Complementary Model balances the strengths of the board and the executive leader, recognizing their complementary roles. Its policy philosophy is collaborative, leveraging the collective expertise of the board and management. The process for policy development involves joint identification of policy needs by the board and the administration, a collaborative drafting process, and final approval by the board with heavy consideration and input by the executive. Key implementation details include regular communication between the board and leadership, flexible role boundaries based on expertise and context, and an emphasis on teamwork and mutual support.

Accountability Measures: In the Complementary Model, the board and administration share accountability. Joint goal-setting and performance reviews are common, with the board and leadership evaluating their collective performance. This model may use balanced scorecards or other tools that measure specific indicators of organizational health. Regular stakeholder feedback mechanisms are often incorporated to ensure accountability to the broader community.

Board-Executive Relationship: This model fosters a strong, collaborative relationship between the board and the executive. It recognizes both parties' unique strengths and perspectives, encouraging open dialogue and collaborative problem-solving. This approach can lead to more innovative solutions and a sense of shared ownership, but it requires clear communication and mutual respect to be effective.

Consensus Model

The Consensus Model provides opportunities for collaborative decision-making and shared responsibility. Its policy philosophy is that policies should be developed through collective agreement, ensuring that all community members have a voice. The policy development process involves issues identified by any board member or stakeholder, open discussions and deliberations involving all board members, and policies adopted only with consensus. Key implementation details include emphasizing participa-

Policy Development

tory processes, decision-making, and a strong focus on building relationships and trust among board members.

Accountability Measures: In the Consensus Model, accountability is often achieved through high levels of transparency and shared responsibility. Because all board members must agree on decisions, their peers hold each member accountable. This model usually incorporates extensive documentation of discussions and decision-making processes. The governance process typically includes regular opportunities for stakeholder input and feedback. The board may also engage in frequent self-reflection exercises to ensure the consensus process works effectively and all voices are genuinely being heard and considered.

Board-Executive Relationship: The Consensus Model often results in a highly collaborative relationship between the board and the executive. The executive is usually deeply involved in board discussions and decision-making, though the board president must ensure their voice doesn't overshadow others'. This model can create strong buy-in and support for the executive's initiatives; however, it may also lead to slower decision-making and potential frustration if the executive feels the need for quicker action.

Carver Policy Governance Model

The Policy Governance model emphasizes clear role separation between the board and the administration. Its policy philosophy is proactive, developing policies to guide the organization's direction and set boundaries for its executive leadership. The process for policy development involves the board developing high-level "ends" policies, the administration developing "means" policies within the board's set boundaries, and regular policy reviews and updates. Key implementation details include a clear distinction between board and management roles, a focus on strategic direction rather than operational details, and an emphasis on board unity and speaking with one voice.

Accountability Measures: The Carver Model emphasizes clear accountability through continuous monitoring of administrative performance. The board sets specific, measurable goals (the "ends") and limitations on administrative authority (the "means"), then regularly evaluates the executive leader's performance in achieving these goals within the set boundaries ("executive limitations"). This model also typically includes regular board self-evaluation against its policies.

Board-Executive Relationship: The Carver Model promotes a clear separation of roles between the board and the executive, leading to a more professional, less personal relationship. The executive has significant freedom to operate within defined boundaries, fostering trust and empowering leadership. The Policy Governance model requires excellent communication to ensure the board remains informed without overstepping its role.

Summary of Key Differences

The key differences among these governance models lie in their approach to decision-making, the relationship between the board and executive, and their focus on accountability and learning.

The Traditional Model offers close oversight but can blur the lines between Governance and management, while the Complementary Model seeks a balance, leveraging the strengths of both board and superintendent. The Consensus Model prioritizes collaborative decision-making but may sacrifice efficiency for thoroughness. The Carver Model, in contrast, provides a clear separation of roles but may create distance between the board and operations.

Regarding board-executive relationships, these range from the potentially micromanaged executive in the Traditional Model to the highly empowered executive in Carver's

Policy Development

Policy Governance Model. The Complementary Model fosters collaborative relationships, while the Consensus Model involves the executive deeply in decision-making processes, which can lead to a rubber-stamp board if the board doesn't establish strong guardrails.

Accountability measures also vary, from the traditional audits and performance reviews in the Traditional Model to the shared responsibility approach of the Consensus Model. Contrast those with Policy Governance, which has consistent, ongoing accountability checks. Ultimately, the choice of model depends on the organization's specific needs, culture, and goals. Many organizations may find that a hybrid approach, combining elements from different models, works best for their unique situation.

« »

Of the previous models, I've used Carver's Policy Governance model the most, and it aligns well with Values-Based Governance. You can check out John Carver's book *Boards That Make a Difference* (2006) to better understand how this model works. The Policy Governance model provides a great starting point if your board wants to increase accountability and focus on values-based policies.

I do not recommend implementing VBG and a new policy model simultaneously. That much change can put too much strain on your district and administrative team, leading to collapse rather than transformation.

I'll conclude the policy chapter here. Many volumes exist on policy and its importance, but it's merely one piece of the bigger scheme of Values-Based Governance. Please review the policy models in this chapter and see which will fit your organization. Policy is an essential tool in your governance toolbox, so ensure you know how to wield it appropriately.

Homework – Chapter 7

1. Imagine you're a board member of a school district that hasn't updated its policies in over a decade. Develop a strategy to review and update the district's policies, incorporating the concepts of operational and governing policies discussed in the chapter. How would you ensure that the new policies reflect the district's current values and needs?

2. Analyze a recent controversial event or decision in your local community or a well-known organization. How might a strong policy framework, developed using Values-Based Governance principles, have helped prevent or better manage this situation? Propose a specific policy the board could implement to address similar issues in the future.

3. The chapter discusses the importance of having a "policy hacker" to test policies for potential misuse or unintended consequences. Design a role-playing exercise where one group creates a new organizational policy, and another group acts as "policy hackers" to identify potential flaws or loopholes. What did this exercise reveal about the policy development process?

Chapter 8:
Cultural Adaptation

Chapter Summary:

In this chapter, you'll learn how to build values into your district's culture by emphasizing accountability and academic outcomes. You'll see practical examples of changing board meeting culture and ensuring congruence between actions and words. By the end, you'll know how to adapt your district's culture to support your board's stated values and mission.

Once you have completed the strategic alignment process and developed/revised the applicable policies to reflect the board's espoused values, you must build those values into your district's culture. Cultural adaptation is not just a step in the process, but a crucial journey that could alter the direction of your district. It's about aligning your district's culture with your desired values; it doesn't necessarily mean you need to change it drastically. The main aspects of culture you should be aware of as we progress through this chapter are accountability, language, and focus.

Cultural adaptation has to start with the board and senior leadership, and accountability has to be the cornerstone of any work around culture. As the guiding force, the board is responsible for holding itself and the Superintendent accountable and for setting the tone for the entire district.

Accountability, as the first attribute of cultural adaptation, plays a dual role in this process. It's not just about holding individuals accountable, but about making accountability an integral part of the culture. The board must hold the administration accountable, ensuring that every action aligns with the district's values and goals.

The second key aspect of cultural adaptation for any school board is ensuring your language is intentional and consistent. The final element is ensuring your board maintains its focus on academic outcomes. This focus should link directly to your district's mission or vision statement. If it's not, it's a sign that your focus may be misplaced. Just as with accountability, the board should lead the way in prioritizing academic outcomes.

Your district administration needs to complete the cultural adaptation process, ensuring accountability is the top priority. You can't focus on student outcomes without accountability measures in place. Then, once the appropriate accountability measures are in place, ensure everyone is focusing their time where it needs to be. These two blocks will significantly change the culture of your board meetings, your district, and your schools.

Agenda Revisions

When I took over as president of my school board, the first thing I did was to take a red pen to the agenda. I'm not speaking metaphorically, either. I sat down with our superintendent, our upcoming agenda, and a red pen. I started adding time limits to each presentation scheduled during the meeting, giving only a few minutes to non-academic, non-student-focused items. I also provided ample time for the presentations on test scores, academic goals, and related topics. As mentioned in Chapter 6, I replaced several presentations with written reports, reducing meeting time while preserving due diligence and public transparency. This fundamental shift in how our board conducted meetings showed the staff that we, as a board, weren't asking them to do something we weren't willing to do ourselves, and it was a radical shift for our time and attention.

We cut the business portion of our board meetings from 2.5 hours to about 75 minutes, and we reduced the number of monthly board meetings, taking the total time from 5+ hours of business each month to less than 1.5 hours. Not only did that force our board to focus on student outcomes, but it also gave time back to the staff. Now, the administration could spend more time supporting the students and teachers in the district and less time creating reports for the board.

This change focused our board's time and allowed our staff to focus on students.

Congruence in Actions and Language

The community will be watching you. When you start making cultural changes in your district, detractors will look for incongruencies to make you look like a hypocrite. That's why these changes must start with the board. Integrity and transparency go hand in hand—without them, you can't drive effective cultural change.

You have to do what you say, and say what you do.

As stated above, irritating the cultural adaptation initiative in the boardroom demonstrates the board's commitment. Make sure to change your actions, where you spend your time, and your language. Language is an integral part of culture. When you begin to use language focused on your outcomes, your community will notice. I promise.

A few months after I started practicing Values-Based Governance, which allowed me to control the district's agenda and language, I sat down with a community member for coffee. She and I had disagreements about many things since my term started, but there was a new issue in the district she wanted to discuss. At one point during our conversation, she turned to me and said, "I don't know what's up with this whole *reasonable* thing you've got going on, but whatever works for you..." And honestly, I was a little taken aback by her comment. I gave her a half-laugh, and we moved on in our conversation.

I spent some time thinking about her comment that afternoon. You see, my values hadn't changed, but my language changed to reflect the board's values and student success consistently. Now, the district focused on greater accountability, leading to a brief period of tumult and turnover among senior staff, as they could no longer get away with the status quo. The district's language had shifted as well. We spent less time focusing on programs and more time focusing on better instruction. Our board meetings changed as outlined above.

We had presentations on student outcomes, as well as 35-minute presentations on how the superintendent was following each specific policy. I kid you not, I remember spending over 30 minutes listening to a presentation about easements around one of our future school sites. Yes, a *future* school site. It was all good and interesting, but our focus wasn't on anything that would impact our current student outcomes. Our focus was on the board.

In contrast, I was now adapting our culture to our outcomes. While still full of good information, we were discussing topics that impact student success. Now these oppositional community members saw that we were operating with transparency and integrity. That's why she thought I was being reasonable. It wasn't that I had changed, but rather the context in which we, the district, were operating had changed.

Focus Where You're Focused

Mike Tomlin, long-time head coach of the Pittsburgh Steelers, has had many quips over the years. One of my favorites is "The standard is the standard." When that first came out, all the analysts and commentators asked, "What is that supposed to mean?" For me, it was apparent.

I played team sports throughout my life, but soccer was my primary sport. As with any activity, you have to practice to get better. In team sports, you have to practice together many times each week. Some players practice harder than others, and those are the players who make the most significant improvement. That level of effort becomes "the standard" for the other players. As a coach and a parent, I want all my players to practice with the same high-level intensity as the top-caliber players.

You have to try as hard as the next guy. You have to do your part to make the whole team better. You must ensure you're not the weakest link on the team, but at the same time, you want to make the weakest link stronger. Practice with intentionality. Play with intensity. That's the standard, and it's the standard.

When you're practicing, your focus should be on getting better. You should take time to work on your mechanics. For soccer, it's ball placement. It's foot planting. It's where and how you strike the ball. It's moving towards space and putting the ball where it needs to go. In games, your focus is on execution. The mechanics aren't going to change much during the game itself, especially if you haven't focused on those during practice.

All that to say, as a board member, you have to remain focused where you're focused. When you say that student outcomes are the most crucial thing in your district, you have to focus on them. You have to make that focus part of your culture. You can only attain goals you've identified, defined, and focused on. I've already discussed how cultural adaptation plays out in the boardroom, but you have to make that outcome your solitary focus throughout the organization.

Pick a target, focus on it, and make it better.

Pursuing Your Targets

For example, if you want academics to improve, you have to invest more in academic instruction. When our district wanted better English Language Arts (ELA) scores, our superintendent led a district-wide book study on literacy instruction. She bought books, led discussion groups (online and in person), and brought in the author for a workshop. She spent time over the summer with building-level leaders, setting the expectation for developing our literacy curriculum.

Our superintendent invested in professional development and focused on our outcomes. Everyone had the same focus, from the board (who joined the book study) to the classroom teachers. We all spoke the same language. We led by example in the boardroom, and the board set expectations for every employee in the district. We kept our focus where we were focused.

In contrast, you can't say you want to focus on math *and* reading. At that point, you've split your focus, and your district will struggle to make progress on either. From a cultural adaptation perspective, leadership must ensure everyone focuses on the same thing. Pick a single subject and earnestly pursue it. Resource your teachers and put explicit expectations around it.

My board struggled with this singular focus. While the district focused on literacy, I had new board members who desired to fulfill campaign promises. I'm all for doing what you said you would do, but their campaigns didn't focus on student outcomes. Their misaligned priorities created conflict because while most of the board was trying to ensure our focus remained on increasing student outcomes, other board members wanted to focus on other issues.

I want to provide a quick caveat before diving into the following example. There will always be times when you have to address urgent matters regardless of how they align with your mission. Depending on your governance model, such as a consensus model, you might need to work with your superintendent to address issues promptly. Other models allow your board to spend a few minutes ensuring your administration addresses the problems. I'm not advocating that your board eschew its responsibilities in handling urgent situations. Now, with that out of the way, let's continue.

Security is an excellent topic for the board to discuss and invest in, but when the board has already focused on academics, then it is the wrong target at that time. When non-academic targets arose, I had to sit down with board members one-on-one to explain why the district and the students needed them to focus on the same targets as the rest of the board. The time to focus on these other issues would come later. As a board, we couldn't expect everyone else to maintain their singular focus if we weren't maintaining ours.

Education is a team sport, and, just as in any other team activity, you have to rely on your teammates to do their jobs. It takes everyone practicing hard, maintaining the standard, and completing their part to ensure success for the whole district. Each staff member has a role to play, and they can't lose their focus. If they do, there are consequences, not for us as a district, but for the students. It's a high-risk game, and everyone must keep their heads about them to succeed. When everyone commits to their role with this level of focus and accountability, culture adapts within your strategic alignment framework.

The board is an integral part of the district's team. You must maintain your singular focus and set the example for the cultural shift.

Goal Work

Goal setting is another key to maintaining your focus. When developing your strategic goals, ensure they align with your district's mission, vision, and outcomes. It takes intentional effort to get everyone working toward the same goal, and having those goals as part of your strategic plan simplifies coordination across the district.

When developing your goals, make sure they align with the outcomes you want. I know that sounds simple, but let me give you an illustration. One district wanted to focus on teacher retention. When the district first developed its goals, the stated metric was no more than 15% attrition per year. That's a good goal, as it attempts to keep your recruiting efforts to a minimum. After a few years of being close without hitting the mark, they rewrote the goal. The new goal was to retain 85% of staff.

Even though the goal is practically the same, notice the subtle difference in how the goal is positioned relative to the desired outcome. Instead of telling people that you don't want staff turnover, they reoriented the goal toward retention. They moved from worrying about a negative impact to discussing the positive aspects. This reframing changes how you talk about the goal and how you work to achieve it, and ultimately, it changes your ability to accomplish the goal.

It's necessary to pay attention to these small details, as each detail matters when you're working to make cultural adaptations that align with your values.

Symptom vs Cause

One thing I've had to caution many boards against is focusing on the symptoms rather than the causes. I ran a Boy Scout summer camp program for a few years in college. It was hot, and we had dehydration issues. Since we worked primarily with young teens, drinking soda was much more intriguing than consuming tepid water.

Our medic, an old Army Ranger, would end up with a line every afternoon of kids complaining about headaches. He'd give them some electrolytes and water and return them to work on their merit badges. The kids would still have a slight headache but recover soon enough. Our medic would joke, "They didn't get a headache for lack of a Tylenol. Those kids simply need more water."

Most districts assume Tylenol is the cure for the metaphorical "headache," treating the symptoms rather than the cause. This mismatch between values and culture is the primary cause of friction that develops into bigger problems over time.

Drop-out rates in high school are a symptom, not a cause. Declining enrollment and increased turnover are symptoms, not causes. Missed minutes for special education students and angry parents at board meetings are symptoms, not causes.

To be fair, some of these cause other problems, but you don't want to try to fix them directly. Your team needs to conduct root-cause analyses and identify the causes to fix them. District culture is often the cause of these issues. Focusing on your outcomes, mission, and values will demonstrate consistency, ultimately building trust and improving your culture.

« »

Ultimately, adapting your district's culture is not always a quick fix; in fact, it rarely is. You'll need to endure some painful times, but the challenges are worth the benefits. Cultural adaptation completes the Values-Based Governance framework. Strategic alignment defines your values, policy development embeds them in your organization, and now cultural adaptation ensures they're lived out daily in every classroom and office.

Applying those values is where the rubber meets the road. All the mission statements and policies in the world won't help students if your culture doesn't support excellence. But when you get culture right, when accountability becomes natural, when everyone focuses on student outcomes, when your values drive daily decisions, that's when transformation happens.

Cultural adaptation is critical to Values-Based Governance and serves as the bridge between good intentions and real results for students.

Homework – Chapter 8

1. Analyze your organization's current culture and its stated values and goals. Identify any misalignments and propose a specific plan to align the culture with the principles of Values-Based Governance. How would you ensure congruence between actions and words throughout this process?

2. Design a board meeting agenda that reflects the cultural adaptation principles discussed in the chapter. Explain how your agenda items, time allocations, and overall structure focus on student outcomes and accountability. How does this agenda differ from a typical board meeting in your experience?

3. Choose a specific goal for your organization (e.g., improving literacy rates and increasing teacher retention). Develop a cultural adaptation strategy to pursue this goal.

4. Identify a recurring "symptom" in your organization (e.g., high dropout rates, declining enrollment). Conduct a hypothetical root cause analysis to determine potential underlying causes. Then, propose a cultural adaptation strategy that addresses these root causes rather than just the symptoms. How does this approach align with Values-Based Governance?

5. Create a communication plan to introduce and reinforce cultural changes in your organization. Include specific examples of how you would use language to reflect your values and desired outcomes at different levels (board, administration, teachers, students, community). How would you measure the effectiveness of this communication in driving cultural adaptation?

Part III:
The Strategies

The model for Values-Based Governance has been discussed and laid out for you, but it only provides a frame of reference. I hope you are beginning to see trends and potential issues within your board. The next portion of this book will focus on strategies to help you do the work of Values-Based Governance. This book and framework won't mean anything if they don't help you identify and resolve problems. This book is a practical guide, and Part III will provide you with some strategies to make a difference and begin governing from your values.

9
nine

Chapter 9:
First Things First

Chapter Summary:

In this chapter, you'll learn how to create the foundational documents that drive Values-Based Governance: mission, vision, shared values, unique value proposition, and the Decision Lens. You'll understand the specific criteria for effective statements and see how these documents work together. By the end, you'll have the tools to build a solid foundation for VBG implementation.

Governing from your values might seem nebulous, but there is a process to this work. Just as Part I laid the foundation for the rest of this book, this chapter is the necessary infrastructure for the remaining strategies. Later work won't be impactful if you don't use the appropriate framing. This chapter details such groundwork.

You can't implement Values-Based Governance without understanding your values. It's that simple. So, you must first define your values as a board and a district. Once you've put those values into words, the rest of the work becomes relatively straightforward, although it won't necessarily be easy.

Foundational Documents

Strategic alignment is when your mission, vision, and core values align with your services, policies, and outcomes. As I like to refer to them, these foundational documents will be your North Star as you make decisions and create policy. Everything you do should point back to these guiding principles. It's critical to develop your mission, vision, and core values practically and methodically so they provide the guidance needed to make decisions.

These foundational documents, specifically your mission, should start with your outcomes. What are you, as an organization, designed to accomplish? As a school district, you exist to educate students. This mantra is the district's primary directive. Everything you do as a district should further that outcome.

Mission

When organizations use the word "mission," they often use it differently from its original or intended meaning. "Mission" comes from the Latin word *missio*, which means "sending." The initial concept of the root refers to a task or assignment given to someone. Over time, the word "mission" has evolved to include broader concepts of purpose, objectives, and tasks.

Let's utilize the original definition. Your mission should be something your staff can rally around. Your teachers, administrators, bus drivers, cafeteria workers, district leadership teams, and everyone else working or volunteering will be standard bearers for your mission. They are being "sent" and need an assignment to carry out. Your mission is that assignment.

With this in mind, you must create a mission that meets your needs. If a district mission already exists, it is essential to examine that statement to see if it aligns with and fulfills the *missio* definition. The board should also consider length, clarity, and focus when evaluating your mission statement.

Your mission statement should be short enough to fit on a business card and readable at arm's length. This exercise speaks to how easy it is to read and recite your mission. Your mission statement should be something all your employees can memorize and report when walking down the hall at a conference. Keeping it short can take time and be complicated. Mark Twain once wrote, "If I had more time, I would have written a shorter letter." This quote alludes to the work the board must do to create a mission statement that captures what you need it to say and keeps it manageable. If it's short and plain enough, your mission statement is a good candidate for internalization. Internalization is how you get your staff to connect with your mission and start to own the results.

Your district's mission needs to be clear. It needs to consist of simple language that everyone in your district will be familiar with and able to use. Education is an industry that prides itself on using acronyms and jargon, which often obfuscates meaning and marginalizes non-educators. Confusing board members with jargon isn't intentional, but your district needs to be the exception. It's important to remember that your district employs a wide range of educational levels. You likely have non-native English speakers in your district, which is another reason to use plain, simple words when communicating. When developing your mission statement, ask yourself whether your middle school students would understand what it means.

Mission statements should mirror the outcomes you want to see in your district. I've seen mission statements where you read them and still don't know what they want to accomplish. Others list four or five desirable outcomes for their graduates. Unfortunately, you can't focus on that many targets. Remember, your mission statement isn't about graduates alone but *all* students. If you focus purely on seniors and why they'll be amazing in college (or a career), you could isolate your elementary teachers. The unintentional isolation of a teacher segment, in turn, could prevent them from internalizing the mission statement and applying it to their students as needed.

Integrating Your Mission

Once you've weighed your existing mission statement to see how it compares, you must decide whether to keep it as is, modify it, or start from scratch. Keeping or modifying is fine, and you can do that work easily. If your board decides to start from scratch, it is best to bring in an external person to help facilitate those conversations. Using an objective facilitator allows your board to focus on the district's results rather than the process.

Part of Values-Based Governance is accountability, and keeping your mission short, clear, and focused will be an advantage when it comes time to set goals for your superintendent. You'll want to ensure the goals align with the district's mission. Then, during the annual evaluation, you'll ensure the superintendent achieved those goals.

One thing to note is that your district will never attain its mission. You will never be able to look back and say, "We did it! Mission accomplished." You will always have more students coming into your system who need help, and your district will still be here in 50 years, still educating students, teaching them to read and solve mathematical equations. Students will always need to learn kindness, resiliency, and teamwork. There will always be more work towards your mission's success.

Vision

Many districts make the mistake of using a vision statement to define a long-term goal. Being goal-oriented can introduce conflict between your mission and vision statements, as both would describe tasks the district needs to accomplish. In an effort to eliminate such conflict, I prefer to define vision by asking, "Why is the world a better place because of our district?" The answer to that question is your vision; it's the realization of a better tomorrow for your community.

This definition aligns with the word "vision," which derives from *visio*, meaning "seeing." This Latin root suggests a mental image or a clear understanding of something that hasn't yet fully materialized. Your job as a board is to cast that vision. What does your community look like in the future because of your organization?

Although it sounds like a long-term goal, you should write your vision statement as a picture. It should still be short, but use words to describe it so that others can see it, too. You still want people to be able to process your statement and recognize it when they see it. Employees don't have to memorize the vision statement like they do the mission statement.

You don't need people to internalize your vision statement because your district will intrinsically attract people who connect to your district once it's defined—new hires will already embrace the vision due to their natural connection to your district. The intrinsic nature of this connection to your district is deeper than any other reason. They'll "know" your vision statement because it aligns with theirs. You're connecting with people who share your vision and working together to create the ideal vision for your community. Your vision statement is a powerful tool for cultural adaptation because it helps anyone in the community, internal or external, understand where you are steering the ship.

Developing and promoting this vision is also a step towards accountability. Everyone in your community will see this vision and adjudicate your decisions/actions based on it. As your actions and policies align with your vision, you will build community support—integrity matters.

Shared Values

Aside from developing your mission and vision statements and ensuring they support the board's work, your shared value statement is the third foundational document. This statement helps align your board and is a tool I've used to help unite boards during conflict.

I became board president after an election cycle brought in two new members. Another member resigned due to changing work obligations, and within six weeks of the election, we had seated three brand-new board members. We all shared similar value systems, but we applied them in two different ways during a particularly contentious issue (which lasted a couple of months, unfortunately).

As this friction developed, I knew my job as president was to bring everyone together. When the board doesn't work harmoniously, the students and district suffer. My responsibility was to get us back on track, rally our group around the mission, and maintain our focus on student success.

One of my values as a leader is initiating reconciliation. A couple of board members were particularly disappointed with how the contentious issues had played out. They believed I wasn't acting in line with my values, which I shared to a great extent with these two members. Knowing this, I set up regular meetings with each of them to focus on our professional relationship. I had lost their trust, and I needed to earn it back.

Reality doesn't matter when times get rough. In their view, I had reneged, which breached our trusting relationship.

The second thing I did was pull together a work session in which we developed a set of shared values. The Shared Values Exercise is a group activity(detailed in Part IV), and everyone had time to share what was important to them. As I already knew, the board agreed with nearly all of the listed values. We spent a few hours working on a single statement encapsulating our shared values.

Besides bringing the board together, this exercise allowed each member to see that we all cared about the same things. We all wanted to pursue academic excellence, steward the district's resources responsibly, and create neutral learning environments that allowed students to focus on academics. We all cared about partnering with parents throughout a student's K-12 career. It allowed all board members to see that, despite some differences in tactics and approach, we were on the same page where it mattered.

Developing this statement also provided accountability for the board and clarity for the administrative team. As a board, if someone starts peddling societal values or group values outside your shared statement, you can pull them back to your board's values. There's now an anchor point where you've all agreed to support and uphold these stated values.

Our superintendent also appreciated this work not only because it helped reduce friction among the board, but also because it provided clarity for her to implement policy. The board's value statement served as a lens for decision-making across the district.

Developing this shared value statement was pivotal to how our board operated, and it contributed to the ongoing success of our students and our district.

Unique Value Proposition (UVP)

Looking around my neighborhood, I can get a cheeseburger at no less than four restaurants within a three-mile radius. Why do I choose one of them over another? Taste, service, and convenience are all factors I consider before making a choice. But the interesting thing is that almost none of them are much different than the others. For roughly the same cost, I can get a burger and fries, and my kids can choose between a cheeseburger or chicken fingers, which is necessary since I have kids who like both. None of these businesses distinguishes itself or explains why I should choose it over the others.

Now, this is a lot like education. Some states allow families to choose a neighborhood school, but many don't. Most states offer some form of charter school option, allowing families to send their kids to schools outside of normal district operations. All states have private schools, though not every family can afford to send their child to one. Regardless of how your state operates, you're fighting for staff from a limited pool of candidates.

All this comes down to how you position yourself compared to other districts and schools in your area. It doesn't matter if you're trying to bring in new families or woo highly qualified staff members. You need to explain to them why your burger and fries are better than all the other options in your community.

To that end, few districts develop a unique value proposition (UVP), which is an oft-forgotten and underutilized tool in every district's toolbox.

Because of limited educational options nationwide, most districts take whoever shows up in their neighborhood. Kids from across town can't be bused in, or even join the district in many cases, so why worry about differentiating your district? The answer is straightforward: you should differentiate your district (or school) because your district is different. The uniqueness of your students, staff, and families needs to be acknowledged and celebrated.

Your UVP is what makes you different from the others. It's a distinguishing factor. Even if you don't post it publicly, it will impact your communications and rhetoric. It's a point of pride for your staff and students to be part of something unique in the community.

I recommend that every district develop a UVP and use it internally. If you're in a place where families have options for where to send their students, you can use it externally as well. Where the shared values statement belongs to the board, the UVP belongs to the district. Your UVP is another factor to help with cultural adaptation. It helps define who the district is and supports staff in understanding how their roles contribute to its success.

The Decision Lens

You have to make many decisions every day. It starts early with, "Do I snooze my alarm or get out of bed?" Then, make another hundred decisions before you leave your house in the morning. Each time you decide, there's a matrix or framework at play. The framework you use is often implicit and goes unnoticed, but you could have an explicit framework for bigger decisions. This matrix could take any form, from a pros-and-cons list to throwing darts at a wall. No matter what decision you need to make, there's some rationale behind your choices.

It's no different for the staff members in your district. They use some framework as a basis for their decisions. These matrices impact policy, curriculum, and innumerable other daily choices in each classroom, building, and district office. Rather than defaulting to an informal decision matrix, VBG introduces the Decision Lens to help you define and formalize the decision-making process, ensuring staff make value-aligned decisions throughout the district.

Values-Based Governance is meaningless if your values stay in the boardroom. You have to get them out into the far corners of the district for them to matter and have an effect. I've seen a lot of frustration from board members when they espouse specific values and then come across counterexamples presented by parents or staff.

Not only does the Decision Lens help ensure values get into school buildings, but it also equips and enables employees to make decisions, enabling the implementation of decentralized leadership. Decentralized leadership, specifically in a school district, is a structure in which decision-making authority is distributed across levels (from the classroom to the district office) rather than concentrated solely at the superintendent's level. This approach encourages individuals closer to the point of implementation to make decisions that affect their specific areas of responsibility.

Introducing a decentralized model is also part of cultural adaptation. Jocko Willink, a retired Navy SEAL, author, and management consultant, stated in his podcast, "Culture is the premier form of decentralized leadership." When you have a strong culture, your team is empowered and authorized to make decisions. They can become leaders without seeking guidance on every little detail. And it goes both ways: a strong culture enables decentralized leadership, and decentralized leadership enables a strong culture.

Giving staff members autonomy and ownership in decision-making can go a long way toward increasing employee satisfaction and reducing turnover.

First Things First

The good news is that you've already completed your Decision Lens by developing your mission, vision, policies, shared values statement, and UVP. Figure 9.1 shows how these foundational documents work to create your Decision Lens.

As you'll see in Figure 9.1, your Decision Lens is at the convergence of all five segments. You empower staff members to choose the best answer that aligns with each of these.

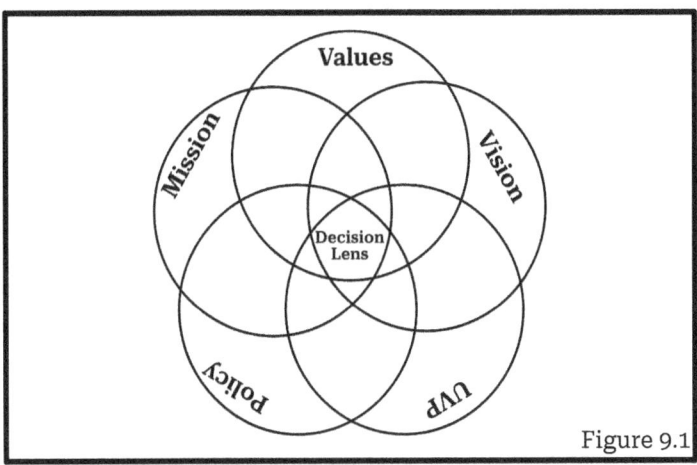

Figure 9.1

If I were to put the Decision Lens into a priority-style format, it would be something like this:

- Is this a real problem or an imagined one?
- If it is a real problem, is the proposed solution legal and ethical?
- If it is both legal and ethical, does the solution move us further from or closer to our mission?
- If it moves us closer to our mission, does the solution align with our vision for an ideal future?
- If it aligns with our vision, does it adhere to relevant policies?
- If it adheres to policy, does the solution align with the shared values statement?

- If it aligns with our values, does the solution leverage our UVP, or is there a similar solution that does so more effectively?

The above line of questioning is straightforward. And once implemented, you can allow anyone in your district to make decisions within their sphere of control. Notice the hierarchical nature of the questions. If it's not legal or ethical, it doesn't matter whether it aligns with your policies (and I hope illegal solutions don't comply with policy). It's okay if your solution doesn't align 100% with your UVP. I would consider it a bonus, but not a deal-breaker.

I've had people question me, worrying about staff members making bad decisions, and I always respond the same way. *How can it be a bad decision if it passes through the decision lens?* It might not be the decision you would have made, which is fine. You have to trust your team. Think hard about this: if any decision aligns with policy, values, and vision and moves you closer to your end goal, what do you have to complain about?

Stitching It Together

Completing these foundational documents is the core, essential work for implementing Values-Based Governance. It sets the cornerstone for all the other work. I hope you can see how the three tenets of VBG are intertwined—there is a give-and-take, with each tenet playing off of and informing the others.

This work is critical. It can be complicated and tedious, but the result is worth the effort—especially when you engage your community for feedback and input as you develop these documents.

It's also highly recommended that you include your superintendent and other senior leadership in this process. Your administration needs to invest in the work you're doing. Including them in these efforts builds trust and transparency. Not to mention, your district administration knows a lot about your students, parents, and staff who are affected by these statements. It's vital to have their perspective, but the board owns the results.

Homework – Chapter 9

1. Draft a mission statement for your organization that meets the length, clarity, and focus criteria outlined in the chapter. How does this compare to your current mission statement?

2. Review your vision statement. Will your current vision statement attract like-minded individuals to your cause? How might you revise it to reflect a better ideal future state?

3. Develop a shared values statement for your board or leadership team. How could this statement help resolve conflicts and guide decision-making?

4. Craft a unique value proposition (UVP) for your organization. How would you use this UVP to differentiate your organization internally and externally?

5. Apply the Decision Lens framework to a recent challenge in your organization. How might the outcome have differed if the board had used this framework initially?

10
ten

Chapter 10: Understanding the "A" Word

Chapter Summary:

In this chapter, we'll discuss the critical skill of accountability—holding yourself, your board, and your superintendent accountable for results. You'll learn the difference between goals and benchmarks, how to create meaningful accountability measures, and how to conduct effective evaluations. By the end, you'll know how to develop a culture of accountability that drives continuous improvement.

One of the most crucial aspects of governance is accountability. You have to hold your superintendent accountable, and you have to hold yourself accountable as a board. In addition, you are held accountable by the community you serve. The voters elected you to serve *all* students in your district, and the parents of those students will ensure you're being fair and doing your job appropriately.

A community member came up during public comment and called me every name in the book, including a few I hadn't heard before. He did it in an even manner, and if you only listened to his tone, you'd think he was a rational, concerned community member. His words, however, betrayed that sense of rationality. This particular community member wasn't upset about a specific situation; he didn't like me and the values I stood for.

A few months later, a fellow board member and I met with a group of parents who wanted to discuss philosophical differences. The gentleman above was in attendance at that meeting. I asked him why he thought his previous comments were productive to the district and student outcomes (because this had happened multiple times). He responded, "It's my job to hold you accountable."

Let's be clear here: calling me names in public because he doesn't like my value system, effectively acting like a 4th-grade bully, is not accountability. I've seen this same sentiment, touting hatred as accountability, in boardrooms across the country. I didn't let him get away with that argument, and neither should you.

I'm all for accountability. I'm a staunch defender of the Constitution, and I believe all citizens should hold government entities to a high level of scrutiny and accountability. Local school boards are no exception. But let's be clear about what it means to be held accountable, and it's not name-calling.

Now, we'll take a deeper look at the details of accountability and see whether it supports my claim that the above situation should not be considered accountability. Once defined, we'll discuss what accountability looks like in school districts.

What is Accountability

Accountability is a principle under which individuals, institutions, and elected bodies are answerable for their conduct, decisions, and performance. It includes an obligation to justify actions and accept consequences in return.

I understand this definition is broad, but it's essential. As a board member, you need to understand your board's and your district's obligations. Accountability isn't a bad word; it should empower each side of the equation. Well-implemented accountability is the bedrock of liberty upon which our founders built this country.

Let's look at a few examples of accountability in your district.

Public Towards the School Board

This orientation is the most commonly misunderstood version of accountability. Many members of the public believe they're holding school boards accountable, when in fact they're not. It's just that community members are upset about the school board's values. Notice that *who* the school board is doesn't factor into our definition. It's only regarding actions taken. That's an important distinction and a defining characteristic.

You must understand that your actions, including inaction, are fair game for public scrutiny. These include the decisions you make as a board member, the votes you cast, statements made in public and private, behavior outside the boardroom, interviews or media appearances, and the list continues, specifically as they relate to your elected duty. Your choice of breakfast cereal at the grocery store is irrelevant to the district's business.

Your inaction matters as much as your action. When you are aware of problems and do nothing about them, the community has every right to hold you accountable for the repercussions of inaction. You'll have a lot of issues thrown your way, some big and some small, and you'll need to have some way of navigating those that are legally defensible. Then, you'll have something you can stand on if adverse results or legal action come against you.

It's also important not to confuse accountability with your rights as a private citizen. You still have your liberties granted in the Bill of Rights—you can still do and say what you want as a private citizen. However, the reality is that everything you do reflects on your position. While you're always a board member in the public eye, you retain your personal rights. Which presidential candidate's sign is in your front yard, for example, is not something related to your district duties and not something your community can hold you accountable for as a board member. The distinction is between your actions as a board member (attending events, making decisions, and public statements about the district) and your rights as a private citizen (political beliefs, personal choices unrelated to district business). The challenge is that people will always see you wearing your "board member jersey," even during personal time.

One example was about 18 months into my term, when I was working from home. My wife and I had helped with lunch duty at my kids' school, and we were off to get a quick bite ourselves before heading back to our home office. While waiting at a red light, a car flew through the intersection and onto a berm, running too wide during a left-handed turn due to high speed.

With bated breath, my wife and I pulled over, waiting for the car doors to open. Five high school girls were in the car. Slowly, the back doors opened, followed by the passenger door. The driver sat still as time ticked by until her door finally opened.

A few other community members had pulled over; one was on the phone with emergency services. While my wife and I were getting out of the car, I heard the community member tell the dispatcher, "Yes, and there's one of our board members here, too." I was acting as a concerned citizen, trying to help in an emergency, but my board-member jersey was still on. Imagine what could have happened if I had just sat in the car, checking email on my phone. I was still a "board member" even when I was trying to have lunch with my wife.

You are never "not a board member" while serving, and you are accountable for your actions throughout the term.

School Board Towards School Board

The second type of accountability is that among the school board itself, including annual self-assessments, but it's more than that. It's also how well you hold to your policies and agreements. Does everyone show up and do their work? You owe it to yourself, your board, and your district to carry your share of the load.

Most of the policy models discussed previously include mechanisms for handling board agreements and self-governance. For instance, in the Policy Governance model, a whole policy section is dedicated to "Governance Policies" (or GPs for short), which directs how the board interacts with and manages itself. It covers meetings, conduct, officer duties, elections, and many other necessary guidelines, and it's a great place to define how to hold each other accountable.

These intra-board policies can include many other issues, such as board members not coming to meetings prepared, not showing up at all, or attending only remotely. These are examples of meeting expectations that these policies would detail. From a conduct perspective, you could capture instances when members write opinion pieces in the local newspaper against the board or the district's policies, or when one member starts bullying another to secure a specific vote. Although not necessarily covered under expectations, these examples would violate codes of conduct or board agreements.

One board I served on created a social contract guiding interactions and intentions with other board members. This agreement existed outside of policy, but it was a valuable tool to keep everyone on the same page. It gave us a metric we could all use to hold each other accountable, and it worked out great.

The board's annual self-assessment is another opportunity for accountability. For this to be truly meaningful, your board has to be honest about the work it's doing. You have to be open and transparent in those conversations. Setting up an annual assessment is a great way to start building self-accountability measures and to set the tone and example for the rest of your district.

A few items to consider would be:

- Do board members consistently follow the agreed-upon code of conduct and meeting norms?
- How well has your board redirected to a shared values statement?
- What percentage of board agenda items directly relate to academics?
- When did the board last change its mind based on student outcome data?
- And on and on the list goes. These are merely a few examples for consideration.

There's no perfect measure out there, but you need to choose something and implement it with fidelity. Remember, you're the example and must model the cultural changes you want to see. If accountability is part of your desired culture, and it should be, then you must be willing to undergo that same scrutiny and self-evaluation process.

There is an objective self-assessment in Chapter 14, which reflects the core tenets of VBG. It focuses on behaviors rather than subjective criteria. A downloadable version is also available in the resources section at ChalkForge.com.

School Board Towards Superintendent

When school boards engage in conversations around accountability, they typically mean the "board holding the superintendent accountable for [fill in the blank]" form. They want the superintendent to do what they want, and it's not always in the district's best interest, which is why it's important to define everything in advance. Going back to the board-to-board accountability model above, you must ensure the agreements and policies are clear. You don't want one board member trying to hold the superintendent accountable to a standard different from the rest of the board's agreed-upon metrics. A single board member requesting something different from the superintendent puts your leadership in a highly tenuous position.

I spoke with one board that, mid-year, asked, "How do we handle our superintendent evaluations?" I shouldn't have to say this, but if you're asking this question in the middle of the year, you're already too late. As with any job, you want to set clear goals ahead of time and hold your employees to them. You can't get halfway through the year and then try to figure out the standard to hold them to. Set the goals up front and early in the year.

In Colorado, state statute requires school boards to conduct an annual evaluation of their superintendent, and a public summary must be available to the community. Even if this wasn't a requirement, it's still a good practice, considering the need for transparency. I once spoke to a gentleman who had a district ask him about outsourcing their superintendent evaluation. That's a terrible idea. How would you like to work hard all year and then have your boss, who has watched you every day of every week, bring in someone from outside the company to evaluate you? It's impersonal, and it would be hard for that evaluation to fairly reflect the work done. You owe it to yourselves, your superintendent, and your community to do that work yourself. I'll discuss the superintendent evaluations and accountability measures later in this chapter.

Mutual Accountability: District and Parents

I'll cover these two perspectives together. The board's composition and values have very few implications for these areas of accountability, but they warrant a few paragraphs in this book. Both parents and the district have high expectations for the other, and specifying those expectations is essential.

Parents are coming to the district for a single purpose: to educate their kids.

I know that sounds simple, but at the end of the day, this is why school districts exist. You have to hold up your end of the bargain and do what's in the students' best interests. Navigating this for all of them can be challenging, as some districts have a few hundred, while others have over 100,000. It's challenging to provide a consistent experience for all students in your buildings every day. That's why policy is so important; you must apply it evenly across the district.

Parents have every right to hold the district and the board (collectively) accountable for their students' academic success. The "accountability measures," if you will, are typically the end-of-year test scores. At that point, parents can see how their student(s) stack up against other students in their school, district, and state. These test scores don't provide much room for the district to hide, which is a good thing.

The district must be ready to implement appropriate remedies if parents call you out for not doing your job. The board must prepare for that fallout in case the district fails a student; however, it will likely fall to the superintendent rather than the board. Still, depending on how the school and district perform, the board might face pushback from community members over parents' concerns about their students' academic outcomes.

At the same time, parents have specific responsibilities, for which the district must hold them accountable. Parents must ensure their students are at school and ready to learn. Parents need to be involved and engaged in their kids' education. Homework, projects, and supplemental reading opportunities are all areas where districts need to partner with parents to help students. Research shows the criticality of reading aloud with young students for literacy development and achievement. Districts can only do so much with the number of students they tend to daily. Parents must partner with the district to shoulder these responsibilities.

I spoke with a board of education member several years ago who was raised by his grandmother. Every day, when he came home from school, she made him sit down and complete his homework. She would demand to see it once he finished it, and he couldn't turn it in until she reviewed it. After this gentleman graduated from high school, he learned that his grandmother had only a 6th-grade education, so she didn't know how to check his work.

It wasn't that she was correcting his homework or approving it, but she was holding him accountable for getting it done. She was completing her responsibilities so her grandson could be successful. After retiring from a distinguished business career, he became a school board member. Accountability is good, and no one should shy away from it.

Both the district and parents must adhere to their responsibilities. You're all on the same team, working together to support student success. You need to act like partners and be okay with holding each other accountable for your respective areas of responsibility.

Benchmarks vs Goals

When board members discuss the need for accountability, they almost always discuss goals. Goals are great, but benchmarks are equally important, although often ignored. You must understand the subtle differences between these two terms before discussing how they can impact accountability measures in your district.

Goals have been ubiquitous in professional contexts for decades, if not centuries. Nearly everyone reading this has heard of SMART goals, an acronym that frames a well-defined goal. Outside of minor variations, the acronym stands for Specific, Measurable, Attainable, Relevant, and Time-Boxed.

Specific refers to the goal's targeted nature; it's not broad or intended to accomplish multiple things. Measurable means progress should be quantifiable, and everyone should know once you've accomplished the goal. Attainable means people can realistically achieve the goal through reasonable effort. Relevance implies the goal is a progression towards larger, strategic blocks that matter to the organization and outcomes defined by leadership, and time-boxed goals have an expiry date.

Goals are great things. You set them, focus on them, work hard, and accomplish them. I love knocking out goals and checking things off my to-do list. Goals play a crucial role in your district. If 65% of your students meet grade-level expectations, setting a goal to improve that to 70% would make sense. Your district would have 1 year to achieve a 5% increase in students achieving grade-level proficiency in the stated subject, which would be a SMART goal, as it checks all of the boxes.

Benchmarks are different. Most importantly, they don't exist in a time box as goals do. They tend to persist over time. By implementing a benchmark, you are setting a standard that becomes a performance expectation staff must meet year after year. As such, benchmarks are longer-term than goals; you state them once, then they continue ad infinitum until you decide to change them. Remember, the status quo is the path of least resistance, so ensure the benchmarks you're setting are the appropriate standard.

Taking a both/and approach to target setting will provide constant pressure on your district to improve. You should set goals every year, focusing on improving student outcomes. Setting a goal "to enhance X by 5%" will keep student achievement and growth scores moving upwards. The board should implement benchmarks to keep the district above a certain level.

Suppose you've attained a certain accreditation rating or accountability score and want to maintain that score/rating over time. You could set the benchmark at Y% achievement and Z% for growth. This performance standard resembles drawing a line in the sand and telling your community, "We won't go below this mark. You can expect this from the district moving forward."

Goals and benchmarks are not just strategic tools, but powerful instruments that can significantly impact student success in your district. By setting clear expectations and reviewing them annually, you foster transparency and drive continuous improvement in student outcomes.

Defining Outcomes

When starting down this path of measurement and accountability, the first step is to define your outcomes explicitly. It's great to have goals, but how do you know when you've reached the end? A comforting GPS voice isn't always waiting to state, "You've arrived at your destination." Your board has to make that determination for itself.

You must answer the question, "How will you measure your results?" for every goal or benchmark you set. Remember that *both* target types require measurability. If you can't look at the goal and know exactly how you'll measure it and when you've arrived, you haven't finished creating your target.

One crucial aspect of this work is choosing the proper measurement tool, which I call your yardstick.

Measuring Results

"You get what you inspect" is a principle that has held over time. Results don't happen by accident. There is a reason and a trail you can follow backward from successful results to a practice someone implemented. Inspection is a key ingredient in the recipe for success. You can't inspect a subjective outcome, especially when each board member has a distinct perspective and set of expectations.

When developing your yardstick, keep it simple and easy to understand. There are many smart people in your district, but you don't want them to have to think hard about what the measurement means. It should only require a quick look to see how you're stacking up against the expected outcome, so spot checks and trend lines become mid-cycle tactics.

The challenge becomes choosing the appropriate yardstick for measuring your progress towards your target. The yardstick you use and how you measure your outcomes will dictate the results you get. You'll achieve what you incentivize and what you measure, so it's incumbent upon you to ensure those things align with the outcomes you want to realize. Awareness of this distinction and asking yourself, "What am I encouraging?" will help you make better decisions.

If you want better scores, you have to come up with a yardstick to measure them. If your board is looking more for growth, make that the yardstick. If you want both, you'll need a way to measure an aggregate score. I prefer not to have too many measurements in place at any given time, as it can unnecessarily complicate the results.

It becomes a difficult balance to strike when you focus on two divergent targets. You'll need to ensure your goals and benchmarks are conducive to pairing before finalizing them with your administration. It's a more effective process to focus on a single element and do it well before moving on to the next goal.

Pick a target and execute. Pick a target and execute. Pick a target and execute.

Framing

When developing your goals, you need to frame them appropriately. I discussed this previously and the distinction between focusing on attrition and retention when developing staffing goals. It deserves a little more time here as well.

It is essential to frame the goal or the benchmark in a positive sense. To understand the need for positive framing, let's look at the difference between light and darkness. If you want to see what's in a dark room, you don't want to "eliminate the darkness," do you? No. You want to "turn on the lights." Frame the goal positively or proactively, with respect to the desired outcomes.

This framing is necessary because there are many ways to eradicate darkness. Framing the target around what you want to accomplish allows you to focus on a specific solution. For example, you could eliminate darkness by using a flashlight, a candle, the screen of your cell phone, or flipping a switch to turn on the overhead lights.

The goal you specify might better align with one of the outcomes or options for illuminating a space. For instance, if someone is sleeping in the corner of the room, a small, targeted light with a red filter might be the best option. You could have an entire group trying to see a game board, which suggests using an overhead light. You might want to read a book, so using a lantern might be the best solution.

Knowing and specifying what you want to accomplish, and framing your goal in a way that clearly defines primary and secondary targets, is the most effective way to define your goals and benchmarks. This goal-setting framework lends itself to a process that allows time to discuss, discern, and decide how to proceed and accomplish your desired outcomes. Rushing through goal-setting and framing is a surefire way to incentivize the wrong things and miss your intended targets.

Evaluations

Earlier in this chapter, I mentioned that you get what you inspect. So far, I've only discussed setting clear, specific goals and expectations. Evaluations are the "inspection" part of accountability. Expectations and inspections are two sides of the accountability coin, and from my time working with school board members, I found the evaluation process to be one of the most significant gaps. This section is where we get to dive in a little further.

The board should complete three primary evaluations every year: one for the board itself and two for your superintendent. The evaluative process takes a whole year to execute effectively, beginning with proper goal setting and ending with a review. Starting the process mid-cycle becomes ineffective and puts undue stress on the overall system. You must allow the affected individuals time to begin making changes throughout the district.

With this in mind, you must set goals early in the year. Calling a board retreat in late spring or early summer is a great way to set these goals and frame the upcoming school year. This retreat provides the superintendent with ample time to plan professional development and make changes necessary to move the needle—the timing of the goal-setting lines up well with the end-of-year evaluations. The sequence could be to review progress toward goals and benchmarks (November), conduct a superintendent evaluation (December), and then set new goals for the upcoming year (May).

Board Self-Evaluations

Boards should conduct their evaluations in public meetings, focusing on behaviors, data, and objective criteria. It would be advisable to have a neutral consultant to moderate the assessment. I've seen it too often: board members do nothing but brag and dote on themselves. Voters elect school board members in most states, and since members often seek re-election, they're quick to boast but avoid self-criticism. Providing evidence of adherence to agreed-upon norms/codes of conduct is a great way to ensure this progresses as an objective process for honestly evaluating the board's effectiveness and how well they're modeling its desired behaviors.

To that end, I've created a board assessment that aligns with the objective nature of Values-Based Governance. I call it the "ABCD Evaluation," which stands for:

- Alignment and Focus
- Behavioral Indicators
- Culture Check
- Data-Driven Evidence

The key here is that this self-evaluation doesn't rely on 1-5 Likert scales and arbitrary questions. Too many board evaluations are highly subjective and give you a score for how well your board is doing. Board evaluations shouldn't be a pat on the back or a time to campaign through highlighting small wins. Your community—and your staff—need to see you perform serious reviews of your performance.

This simple tool asks pointed questions, and you'll discover how engaged your board is and how well it's serving your community. Use this evaluation every year as part of your self-evaluation cycle. All you have to do is be better the next time you take this self-assessment.

Let's take a look at the questions in this tool, broken out by section. While we go through these, actually think through the answers to these questions. It is an excellent opportunity to conduct a self-assessment for you and your board.

I have the complete measure in Chapter 14 as one of the resources. If you'd like to use it with your board, it's available for free in the resources section at ChalkForge.com.

First up is the section on "Alignment and Focus." You'll notice how the questions here allude to your foundational documents, truly covering the "Strategic Alignment" side of VBG. The questions are as follows:

- Can every board member recite the district's mission from memory?
- When did you last make a decision using the Decision Lens process?
- How often does the board communicate with the community?
- When you do communicate, what percentage aligns with your foundational documents and supports student achievement?

As you can see in the above questions, you want to provide objective answers. If you expect your staff to use the Decision Lens, you should use it yourself. If you want staff to know the mission, you should memorize it. It isn't purely a function of modeling, but if you're going to use it in practice, you shouldn't have to look it up each time.

Understanding the "A" Word

The second section focuses on behavioral indicators, which I designed to examine how well your board models desired behaviors for your community. Take a look at the following questions:

- How many board members attended the last graduation ceremony?
- How many school events have board members attended in the past year?
- When did the board last change its mind based on student outcome data?
- How engaged is each board member during your meetings? Are members on their phones during the meeting?
- Do board members consistently follow the agreed-upon code of conduct and meeting norms?

These questions focus on behaviors that engage your community. They demonstrate engagement levels with board meetings. Don't underestimate the impact these actions have on your community. Students, parents, and staff pay attention while attending school events, and although board members' absences may not cause large ripples, attendance at these events is recognized and appreciated.

The third section, Culture Check, is where you evaluate how well your board's culture aligns with the culture it desires. Remember, your board is the thermostat: it sets the expectation, and the rest of the district must conform. Are your words and actions aligning? Think about that as you review the following set of questions:

- Would your superintendent describe the board as supportive partners or obstacles?
- Do staff members approach board members with ideas, or avoid them?
- How does your community generally view the school board?

These questions are more subjective, but your experience reveals the truth. The answers to the above questions can lead to misalignment between your words and actions. It's a warning light that you'll need to address on your own.

The final section of the self-evaluation is Data-Driven Evidence. I designed the following questions to be specific data points that you can review and look at data that points to culture. Review the following:

- What was the trend in student achievement in your district over the past three years?
- How many superintendents has your district had in the last five years?
- What percentage of board agenda items directly relate to academics?
- What has been your employee retention rate over the past three years?
- Are there trends from exit-interview data?

Student achievement trends and board agenda items are great ways to ensure you're putting your money where your mouth is. In Part II, I mentioned the need to model culture for your entire community. The Culture Check section above highlights culture issues, and the questions in this section apply data to that modeling behavior.

Finally, looking at superintendents and employee retention can provide insight into cultural issues. Note that turnover isn't necessarily bad if the detractors are leaving. I spoke with a board that witnessed turnover among long-standing employees and families. They recognized how this revealed cultural issues they needed to address. Rather than shrugging and saying, "Oh well." This board investigated the problems and resolved them quickly.

This example demonstrates a great board culture. I hope every board has the self-awareness to recognize who it is and address deviations with urgency.

Superintendent Evaluation Process

For the superintendent, I recommend conducting two evaluations each year. Typically, these are summative and formative evaluations, which are commonly referred to as end-of-year and mid-year, respectively. The formative, or mid-year, evaluation is a spot check and usually happens over the summer. It lets the superintendent know if they're on the right track or need to shift over the remainder of the cycle. This review typically includes policy adherence, academic growth, and progress towards annual goals.

The board should conduct the summative, or end-of-year, evaluation near the end of the calendar year. This cadence gives you time to find a new superintendent if needed and allows your current superintendent time to find a new job. It's respectful for both sides. This evaluation must focus on goals, benchmarks, and student outcomes. Having the summative at the end of the calendar year will allow enough time to receive the data, process it, and make decisions.

If your state allows, it is advisable to conduct both superintendent evaluations in a confidential or executive session. The privacy provided through the executive session gives you, as the board, the opportunity to engage in candid conversations about the superintendent's performance. I recommend starting with just the board, taking some notes, and then bringing the superintendent into the discussion afterward. Take as long as needed because this is meaningful dialogue.

I also recommend making this more of a conversation than simply inundating the superintendent with information. The board and superintendent should already have established trust. Extend that trust by allowing the superintendent to respond, even when delivering critical feedback. This approach works whether the feedback is positive or corrective.

Once the confidential portion of the review is complete, the board owes the community a public discussion of the superintendent's evaluation. Use notes about the superintendent's performance over the year and call out a few specific instances, good and bad, as necessary. Providing an honest summary of the evaluation will show your community and staff that you take your role as an evaluator seriously.

Evaluation Tool

I've seen many boards overcomplicate the superintendent evaluation process, producing 60+ page documents filled with praise and critiques of the superintendent's performance over the past year. Some boards use the evaluation process to pull a "gotcha" moment on their employee and grandstand to bring their tenure to a quick end. Others have used the process to build confidence and community support, practically fabricating achievements to bolster the superintendent's credibility. Neither of these trends results in productive evaluations.

To support simple, objective evaluations, I've created a single-page superintendent evaluation template that follows the 4 A's Framework, which aligns with the tenets of Values-Based Governance. The 4 A's are:

- Academic performance of students
- Attainment of growth and achievement goals
- Adherence to policy and expectations
- Associations with the community

The evaluation template covers all critical data and provides an easily digestible format for presenting it. It is shown in its entirety in Chapter 14 as one of the resources. If you'd like to use it in your district, it's available for free in the resources section at ChalkForge.com. No matter which tool you use, I recommend reviewing and evaluating top goals with acceptance thresholds, student data/outcomes, and then narrative strengths and areas for improvement.

Academic Performance

The first A is Academic Performance. In this section of the evaluation, the board will assess the district's overall academic performance. A few data points to consider are the grade-level performance by year. Is it trending up or down? Note that not all grades will see increases year-over-year, so I recommend looking at 3-year trends. The Academic Performance section should be a review of the district's snapshot, including the district's state ranking and accreditation status.

Figure 10.1 shows the portion of the 4A's template relating to Academic Performance. As you can see in the image, I've kept it pretty simple. Math and English Language Arts (ELA) are the only two subjects listed with the straightforward question: Did it increase, decrease, or remain the same?

1. Academic Performance			
Math:	Increase	Decrease	Stagnant
ELA:	Increase	Decrease	Stagnant

Figure 10.1

Again, this is merely a snapshot of overall performance trends. The next A—Attainment of Growth and Achievement Goals—is where your board should dig into the details a bit more. As discussed earlier in this chapter, you can't have too many goals at any time and reasonably expect to attain them. It's reasonable that you could decrease in one subject area here, but still attain your goals under the second A. This section merely provides a snapshot of district performance trends.

Attainment of Growth and Achievement Goals

The second A focuses on whether your superintendent achieved their goals. As discussed in this chapter, these goals are among the most effective ways to have a significant impact on your students. Creating the right goals, with proper framing and metrics, puts positive pressure on your superintendent to perform. Not all of these need to be academic, but I recommend you lean heavily toward academic-focused goals in this section.

---

2. Attainment of Growth and Achievement Goals
Top Priority Goals:

-
-
-

Were all goals met?	Yes	No
If not, were they critical misses?	Yes	No

Figure 10.2

Figure 10.2 shows the respective portion of the evaluation template. First, the board will recount the three primary goals given to the superintendent. Write them out in the space provided.

For the top goals, these should have been developed early in the evaluation cycle and agreed to by both your board and your superintendent. For each of these goals, you'll want to set acceptance thresholds, which I define in three buckets: Goal Met, Missed, and Critical Miss (discussed in more detail below).

After writing the goals down, the next question is straightforward: were all the goals met? This question is simply seeking a binary response, yes or no. If the goals were not all met, move to the final question: Were any of the missed goals critical misses?

Goal Met. A met goal is anything that meets or exceeds the agreed-upon level. For instance, if your board wanted to see

3rd-grade reading scores improve by 6%, anything over 6% meets the target. It wouldn't matter if it just meets the target number, or if your district knocked it out of the park by another 4%. The district met the goal.

Goal Missed. A missed goal would be anything that didn't meet the success criteria but wouldn't qualify as a critical miss.

Critical Miss. Critical misses are anything your board would deem outside of the standard expectation. Suppose you wanted 85% of your staff to complete a culture and climate survey. A threshold of 80% would be a miss, and anything below that would be a critical miss.

Your board will need to develop these thresholds ahead of time, so the results of the evaluations don't appear to be arbitrary in nature.

Adherence to Policy and Expectations

The third section of the superintendent evaluation is to acknowledge the superintendent's adherence to policy and expectations.

3. Adherence to Policy and Expectations		
Were all policies followed?	Yes	No
Were all stated expectations met?	Yes	No

Figure 10.3

As you'll see in Figure 10.3, all you're doing here is marking "yes" or "no," based on the superintendent's performance. This area shouldn't be a surprise, as the board should provide feedback to the superintendent throughout the year. Many of the policy models discussed in Part II specify processes for ongoing monitoring of policy adherence.

Associations with the Community

The fourth A is a combination of internal and external relationships and how your superintendent represents the board and the district. Figure 10.4 shows five groups I recommend evaluating. Although this list doesn't represent every stakeholder or external group, it provides a strong, broad base for evaluating the superintendent.

4. Associations with the Community			
Students:	Good	Improve	Neutral
Parents:	Good	Improve	Neutral
Teachers:	Good	Improve	Neutral
Taxpayers:	Good	Improve	Neutral
Businesses:	Good	Improve	Neutral

Figure 10.4

Notice these are sweeping generalizations. These are broad strokes over large swaths of people. Some districts use stakeholder groups to maintain connections with different populations, while others handle it more organically. The organic nature of relationships with stakeholder groups can lead to "squeaky wheel syndrome," in which districts often ignore or forget these groups until there's a problem.

When evaluating your superintendent, I recommend a proactive, long-term approach to engaging your community. Don't get myopic and think "We're good to go," simply because your superintendent meets with a group of students every month. Zoom out, request survey responses if needed, but ensure you're giving it a hard, honest look.

Narrative Section

Finally, I've included a narrative section that provides an opportunity to go deeper and provide feedback outside the binary nature of the previous sections. The 4As are restrictive for a reason—we want an objective measurement tool. However, there needs to be space to provide additional information, as shown in Figure 10.5.

There are three sections here: Areas of Strength, Areas for Improvement, and Areas for Follow-up. The first two sections are simply there to make commendations regarding your superintendent's performance. What have they

Understanding the "A" Word

done above and beyond what an average administrator would have done? Don't just state, "They sent out emails to the board every week. They've got great communication skills." The board should expect weekly updates from the superintendent, not commend them for it. You're looking for performance above the average.

Areas of strength:	Areas for improvement:

Areas for follow-up/Action items:

Figure 10.5

It's crucial to track positive traits about your superintendent in this narrative as well. You want to build a culture of accountability, but if you don't acknowledge what the superintendent does well, the evaluation process becomes punitive. That's not the intent here. The evaluation process needs to be an exercise in objectivity, providing feedback on both the good and the bad. If you want a culture of staff appreciation built into your district, you must start at the top and model the behavior of appreciating your superintendent.

The second part lists areas for improvement, listing issues that have arisen throughout the year and that the board has previously addressed. Maybe your board is struggling to get board packets on time, or your superintendent hasn't been communicating well with all of your board members. This section is a great place to track those concerns.

It is vital to list anything here that could become a future goal. Tracking it as an area for improvement provides a paper trail if you end up in an early termination scenario. By documenting these concerns and converting them into formal goals, the board creates a clear record that shows either the superintendent's progress or their refusal to make necessary changes.

The final section, Areas for Follow-up, gives the board space to document next steps, upcoming priorities, and any action items from the evaluation.

« »

The tool above can be used as-is or adapted to your district. I strongly urge you to keep all 4 As intact, as this provides focus on the critical aspects of the superintendent's role. Don't let the evaluation get so long that it becomes redundant, punitive, or irrelevant. Keep it short and objective.

Remember, the evaluation process is not just a formality, but a critical step in embedding accountability throughout your organization. It serves as a cornerstone of your culture, helping to align it with the standard of accountability. When executed effectively, this process enhances transparency and instills confidence in your district's leadership and board. It's an investment of time that yields countless benefits.

Own Your Results

In the vein of transparency, you have to present the end-of-year results to the public. Good, bad, or otherwise, you owe it to your constituency to be honest about your progress. Let your community know if you achieved the predetermined goal and met the benchmarks. On the other hand, if you didn't meet your performance metrics and met a mere 10% of your goals for the year, you should also let your community know.

Hiding information from your community doesn't help. These goals are public records, so anyone in your community should have access to the targets you set and how close you were to achieving them. Sweeping them under the rug because you didn't meet the expectation erodes trust in

Understanding the "A" Word

your community, and it begs the question, "What else is the district trying to hide from us?" I've seen districts set up dashboards that are regularly updated and publicly show the district's progress. Admittedly, showing progress when you get annual data dumps can be hard, as you have to analyze the data and make it digestible. Consider the implications of pushing out a dashboard without narrative information before deciding whether to use it.

The reality is your district earned the results it received. Whether you like them or not, your district earned the grade it received and the results it attained. Just like the students sitting in classrooms across your district, they've earned their grades, too. If my kid got a D on a paper, he earned it by not executing appropriately. Similarly, if he received an A, it shows that he worked hard, took time to review his drafts, edited them a few times, and achieved the appropriate score. Remember that communities judge districts by results, not effort.

At the end of the day, demonstrating your understanding of your role and the need for transparency will provide clear accountability to your community and stakeholders. You build tremendous trust and goodwill when you voluntarily show results. It's taking ownership of the results you earned. The district willingly and deliberately holds itself accountable so the community doesn't have to.

Taking ownership of your results sends a powerful message from the district and goes a long way with your stakeholders.

Homework – Chapter 10

1. How can you frame one of your current district goals in a more positive, outcome-focused way? What impact might this reframing have on achieving the desired result?

2. Design a simple "yardstick" to measure progress towards a key academic goal in your district. How will this measurement tool help in evaluating success?

3. Outline a plan for conducting a mid-year superintendent evaluation that balances confidentiality with transparency to the community. What key elements will you include?

4. Describe a specific way your board can hold itself accountable between annual self-assessments. How might this improve board effectiveness?

5. Draft a brief public statement acknowledging a missed district benchmark. How can you communicate this transparently while maintaining stakeholder confidence?

6. Review the 4As evaluation framework (Academic Performance, Attainment of Goals, Adherence to Policy, Associations with Community). Which of the 4As does your current superintendent evaluation emphasize most? Which needs more attention? How would implementing the 4As framework change your evaluation process?

Chapter 11:
Sustainable Change

Chapter Summary:

In this chapter, you'll learn how to make lasting changes that survive beyond your term on the board. You'll understand the role of culture and policy in creating sustainable change, and learn strategies for building trust while implementing difficult reforms. By the end, you'll know how to make changes that benefit students for years to come.

I've repeated two mantras throughout this book: "Leadership is doing the right thing, especially when it's hard," and "The status quo is the path of least resistance." Both of these phrases are important to internalize because they converge when it's time to make a change in your district.

Change is hard. Most people, especially in education, don't like change. Rather than cleanliness, stability is next to godliness (although cleanliness comes in a close third). I have met educators who have taught in the same room for over 20 years. I've met administrators who have made teachers change rooms to keep staff members on their toes. Despite the difficulty and pushback, change is necessary. You don't make progress when you continue doing the same things over and over.

I was helping coach my kid's soccer team once, and they were coming off a significant loss. I ran them through drills for the entire practice. Towards the end of practice, one of the kids asked when we would scrimmage, and I said we wouldn't. As you can imagine, the kids sighed and slumped, and none of them were pleased with me. The head coach asked the team, "Did you like the last game? Was it fun to lose like that?" All the kids said, "No."

Then, the coach approached the team huddle and said, "If we want different results in our games, we have to change how we practice. We have to focus on the fundamentals and play with more intensity. We'll have time to scrimmage later, but we must practice differently now to play differently later."

I couldn't have conjured up a better story to make my point here. To perform better, you need to change your practices. Start small, get the basics right, and move forward. Change isn't always fun because you may not get to scrimmage, but to play better and win games, it's necessary.

Leadership is doing the right thing, especially when 9-year-olds want to scrimmage.

Know Thyself

Socrates believed that self-knowledge was an essential trait, and he is attributed with the quote, "Know thyself." Knowing your district is the first step in making organizational changes. Proper change management begins with honest self-reflection and evaluation.

When responding to board members' requests regarding policy or process, I always ask, "What is the problem you're trying to solve?" I have no issue making changes and advocating for doing things better, but there has to be a clearly defined reason or problem you're trying to resolve to make effective change.
You can't solve problems you can't define.

Sometimes, the issue people are trying to fix differs from the process they're actively changing. This conflict between intent and impact goes back to the last chapter on accountability and evaluations, where you must ensure you're incentivizing the right things. The same process applies: you need to ensure the proposed solution actually resolves the defined problem. Although this approach is simple, you should make certain the incentives and accountability measures built into the solution push you towards the desired goal. It's a time investment for more impactful change.

This awareness, or "knowing thyself," is a critical first step in the Values-Based Governance process. That's why you have to define your outcomes, mission, vision, values, and UVP up front. This foundational work helps you understand your organization's identity before engaging in any change process. Remember, the focus is on cultural adaptation rather than forcing cultural changes. You need to know where you are and where you want to go, and then create the road map.

As with GPS, the first step is to understand your current location. Once your location is captured and set, the device will look at your destination and provide the route. Based on traffic patterns or wrong turns, the GPS will continually adapt your route to keep you on track. I remember my old dash-mounted unit back in the mid-2000s would say, "Recalculating..." whenever I veered off the designated route. You won't find a better example of cultural adaptation.

So, before you start making drastic changes and focusing on long-term impact, you must know where you are. You have to define the problems that you need to solve. Then you'll rank the issues by their impact on achieving your outcomes. All that's left is to develop your action plan and execute it.

All this starts with knowing your organization and defining your problem.

Lasting Change

Once you've defined the problem and put an action plan in place, you'll likely consider how this change can be sustainable. How do you keep these changes after completing your term on the board? These are great questions, and they're challenging to answer. First, know you're not alone in trying to figure this out. Second, you can't.

I don't mean to be a downer, but the reality is that the next board can make changes just as easily as you can. It's hard to cement things into place, but you can make it difficult or painful for them to do so. Codifying changes in specific ways will force a more public reversal of the policies you implement. It can still happen, but you can force future boards to make those changes in broad daylight, which can be a big win for you.

There are two primary ways to make change "sticky": culture and policy. It's no coincidence that these two ways of handling change are two core tenets of Values-Based Governance. Let's dive a bit deeper into these two tenets, specifically in the context of long-term, sustainable change.

Culture

Culture is critical when you want to make lasting change. I've already discussed cultural adaptation, but I want to explain its implications here. The district's mission, vision, values, and UVP drive culture. Like the Decision Lens, your organization's culture will determine how and why things get done.

I remember walking into work as a young professional, taking the initiative to do something, only to hear, "That's not how we do things around here." This is quintessential culture. It's not necessarily good or bad; it's simply what culture does. Culture creates parameters around actions, initiatives, and rhetoric. When you intentionally adapt your board's values, you modify the DNA of your district's culture.

These cultural shifts become long-term changes because they embed themselves in the organization. District culture drives decisions and behavior. As the board, you're setting the example for the entire district. You have to embody the cultural changes you want to make throughout the organization. Once the board sets the values, the superintendent must take the torch and pass it along to the rest of the district through a trickle-down effect.

After the superintendent passes it along to the administrative team, that leadership group will pass it down to building administrators, who will pass it on to building-level staff. This continuum of accountability becomes an imprint of the board's values throughout your district. Once that dissemination is complete, cultural changes become part of your accountability structure. When people are held accountable for decisions that reflect the board's culture and values, you win the long game.

It becomes increasingly complex for the next board to implement sweeping changes once you reach critical mass in the cultural adaptation game, especially when the focus is on student success. It's not impossible, but it becomes increasingly challenging over time. Cultural adaptation is one of the best ways to impact your district for years to come.

Policy

The other side of cultural change is policy, which is another way to instill value changes in your district. As discussed previously, there are two main types of policy: operational and governing. Operational policies typically focus on specifics, procedures, and related matters, and the board sometimes oversees them rather than the administration. Governance policies primarily focus on values. The board should control these values-focused policies.

The board can strategically use these governing policies to accomplish its work. To see how the two play together, you must understand their relationship. Operational policy must align with governing policy. Whenever a change to governing policy occurs, the administration must revise operational policy to ensure it does not conflict with the new governing standards. A simple example would look like this:

A board wants to ensure that teachers don't make political statements in classrooms, so it enacts a policy stating that all classrooms remain neutral zones where students can focus on their academics. An operational policy currently allows teachers to display a small collection of personal items and mementos, provided it doesn't exceed 9 square feet. The administration must amend this operational policy to comply with the new governing policy.

From here, there are two different ways this could go. The district could amend the operational policy to allow only non-political items, or rescind it entirely and prohibit all personal displays. The safest path would be to revoke the personal display policy because otherwise, the district would become the arbiter of political speech, which is a dangerous position for the district to be in. The best policies eliminate opportunities for bias.

So, with the board focused on making values-based policy changes, you can instill these values in both governing and operational policies. Embedding values in policy requires any future changes to go through the same public change process you're using. However, future boards can still reverse course. So the question becomes, how do you make it harder for them to reverse these policies? The short answer: frame them appropriately.

When framing values-based policy changes, ensure they reflect your mission, vision, and values. Your mission aligns with the organization's outcomes, which, for a school district, are student success. The vision is painting a picture of an ideal future, which you've used to bring aligned individuals into the district. Your shared board values align with student success and whatever else the board deems essential. This process applies your Decision Lens to policymaking.

Imagine how difficult it will be for the next board to make radical changes and publicly undo policies you've implemented that talk about student success and empowering parents. It becomes a long-term public relations game in which your board gets credit for instilling values widely supported by your community. The next board looks silly and out of touch when they try to tear down those policies. This framing is one of the most critical pieces of a well-formed policy.

The Subtle Art of Change

As mentioned previously in this chapter, when engaging in systemic change, you must prepare for conflict. People are happy to stick to familiar things, so if you come in and start advocating for widespread changes, you'll have difficulty winning friends and influencing people.

You need to start with relationships and work to build trust with your leadership team. Remember that your superintendent and senior leadership will be in the trenches to accomplish the board's desired outcomes. It's difficult for them to execute with fidelity without a trusting relationship with the board.

Likewise, ensure you always speak well of the people in your organization. Because your staff members are the ones implementing the board's mission and vision, the board must support *all* staff members. The rub exists when board members criticize teachers—speaking ill of their intentions and tactics—then expect those same teachers to embrace each policy change. That approach kills the culture and morale in your buildings. And in my experience, 95-98% of teachers are focused on student success. They simply want a board that will also support students, rather than playing political games. They want alignment from the dais to the classroom.

Focusing on the right things and coming from a shared values perspective will be invaluable for building trust. Showing that you care about student outcomes and success will go a long way in helping you build trust with staff members. Ask staff members for their names, backgrounds, and the support they need from the district to serve students in their buildings. You'd be surprised how disarming this can be, especially if you ask genuinely and can help ease some issue or frustration they're experiencing.

However, no matter what you do, it will not always be bubble gum and rainbows. Before starting on any journey, it's essential to understand your risk points. Going down the path of implementing Values-Based Governance is no different. The status quo is one of your major risk points, which shouldn't surprise anyone. Anytime you initiate

Sustainable Change

something new, it introduces friction into the system. Don't let that bother you; this is an expected side effect. Remember, you must prepare for the turbulence.

The best way to do this is with tenacity and determination. Buckle up and get ready. Stay laser-focused on the results and outcomes. Make sure you keep your outcomes, mission, vision, and values at the forefront of all your interactions, behaviors, and decisions during your time on the board. You'll need to grow some thick skin quickly because these changes can be emotional, leading people to say mean and hurtful things.

But the good news is that you can do it, and it's worth it. Change is hard, but don't let that deter you from doing the right thing. Focusing on culture and policy will ensure long-term, sustainable change for your district.

Homework – Chapter 11

1. Identify a current problem in your district. How can you reframe it to align with your district's mission, vision, and values?

2. Describe a cultural change you'd like to see in your district. What actions can you take as a board member to model this change?

3. Draft a brief policy that reflects one of your district's core values. How does this policy support long-term, sustainable change?

4. Outline a strategy to build trust with your district's leadership team as you introduce a significant change. What key elements will you include?

5. Identify a potential "risk point" for implementing Values-Based Governance in your district. How can you prepare to address this challenge?

12
twelve

Chapter 12:
Other Key Strategies

Chapter Summary:

In this chapter, you'll discover additional tools for effective board leadership, including how to lead from the minority position, communicate strategically, and ask the right questions. You'll learn practical techniques for building relationships and influencing outcomes even when you don't have majority support. By the end, you'll have a complete toolkit for Values-Based Governance in any situation.

The previous three chapters have focused on implementing Values-Based Governance, providing strategies, and discussing the importance of each VBG tenet. These are sufficient to get your district focused on student outcomes and to align your board's values with the district's culture. In most cases, what I have presented throughout this book will get you where you need to go, but a few more strategies will help you along the way. Those additional strategies will be the focus of this chapter.

Leading From the Minority

The term "minority" often conjures up partisan imagery and legislative bodies. That's not what we're talking about here. I'm referring to the ideological minority of any given board. You can still be a leader even when most people don't think like you. You might not accomplish everything you're trying to do, but you can still make progress toward the desired outcomes.

Policy and Board Action

You can lead from the minority in two primary ways: block bad policies and advocate for good ones.

Being a blocker can give you a reputation as a non-team player. I suggest you handle your opposition with grace to avoid such a reputation. I've accomplished this on my boards by focusing on shared values rather than specific outcomes (I prefer outcomes when in the ideological majority). I sat on a seven-member board, where my perspective represented two votes. This board started pushing ideologies I disagreed with, including enshrining them in the organization's core values.

Rather than calling them names or pitching a fit, I approached it by talking about shared values. I asserted a core truth I knew everyone would espouse, as it was a good, aspirational idea: "I'm sure each of you believes in [insert

Other Key Strategies 195

common value]." Each of the other board members nodded in assent. I knew that once they assented, they wouldn't be able to express opposition to my proposal, since they had publicly accepted the premise of a shared value.

One of my favorite tactics when leading from the minority was to challenge the premise. I'd ask, "Why are we doing this?" and force an explanation. I didn't say it in a nasty way, but I honestly tried to understand. "Help me understand why..." is one of the most valuable phrases in your arsenal. Not only does it gain you sympathy as a team player, but you also get to understand the thinking that brought forward the proposed solution. Then you must poke at one of the weaker connections and steer it in a different direction. It's effectively picking at a scab from an ideological perspective.

Advocating for good policy is much like blocking the bad stuff, but it's a proactive approach. You must start with shared values and make connections from where you are to where you're going. It's the same playbook we discussed previously with long-lasting changes. Know where you are (common value), know where you want to go (good policy or strategic goal), and then formulate your arguments to get from one place to the next.

In Chapter 4, I discussed how I shifted a non-discrimination policy. I did so by using the tactics above and steering the board towards a more sound policy stance. The policy wasn't ideological—it was pragmatic, protecting both board and district. Since the board adopted it years ago, no one has contested it.

This non-discrimination policy was an example of both blocking bad policy and advocating for sound policy simultaneously. It was pivoting. I knew I couldn't prevent the policy from passing or being enacted. Rather than grandstanding, as many in the minority choose to do, I turned it into something less bad and more productive for the district by using our shared values and focusing on the district's stated outcomes. This focus helped establish my reputation on the board as a team player who cared about the district itself. It helped dispel rumors by showing that I operated out of principle rather than partisanship.

The Power of Relationships

Another way to lead from the minority is to build relationships with the administration. I typically collaborate with the administrative team. You want to coach and empower them to make the best principle-based decisions for your district. You can establish yourself as a thought partner.

You'll remember from before that my district used Carver's Policy Governance model, which requires the superintendent to bring reports detailing how they've followed policy over the last year. Once, when we'd brought in a new superintendent, I told her I would vote against the clean report she would present at the board meeting, as I believed there had been a violation during the monitoring period (previous 12 months). She'd been in the role for two months at this point.

She called me and asked for clarification, so I explained my rationale. I coached and taught her how to use our governance model more effectively during the conversation. Within the Policy Governance model, there are definitions of the superintendent's interpretation of governing policy. Not only was this administrator new to our district, but she was also new to Policy Governance. My conversation helped her understand the model, and it empowered her to take ownership of the policies and reports.

Ultimately, after that discussion with her, she started coming to me for advice and clarifications, even over the more tenured board members. I had shown a certain level of expertise and that I cared about her success in this district. I was also willing to coach her and empower her to help ensure her success and that of the district. That was the most influential moment for our relationship during the two years we worked together.

In another situation, the district had developed a strategic plan before our board was seated. The majority of the board disputed one tenet in the plan. Two colleagues sat with the superintendent and told her, "This is bad, and I want it changed." And they had every right to do that. However, this wasn't an effective path forward.

When I had a one-on-one meeting with her, I explained that this tenet was at odds with the character traits we wanted to build in our students. I talked through how it was damaging to our students, and using our shared values, I reframed that tenet to focus on positive character traits.

It took several months, but ultimately, she championed the change within the organization and removed the problematic language from our strategic plan without any fanfare. The district completed the change, set new goals to support the updated language, and presented the changes to the board at a public meeting.

The process went as smoothly as it did because I'd taken time to build that relationship and demonstrate my partnership with her while sitting in the ideological minority. I had proven my involvement in the superintendent's success by explaining how to apply the board's values through policy. Other board members had wanted to resolve issues through directives rather than communicating from a values-based approach.

Communication

Deliberate, intentional communication will help you work through many challenges in your district. *How* you talk about what's going on is just as important as *what* you talk about. This effort goes for board meetings, speaking to staff members, or interviews you may conduct with media outlets. Ensuring your whole board uses consistent language will make a big difference in the overall presentation, especially when it matters.

I've long been a proponent of working through talking points with your entire board before you enter the public domain. This proactive approach lets you align on messaging and iron out any issues. You want to inspect your talking points from several angles.

- How will supportive parents react? How about parents who are opposed?
- What will the staff think about your language?
- Will there be a difference between teachers and administrators in how this is received? What about taxpayers and homeowners in your district?
- Who will be the most advantaged or disadvantaged? How will they react?
- Will this impact student outcomes? If so, will the effect be positive or negative?
- Some board members forget that students listen to board meetings. How will your messaging, behavior, and discussions impact them?

These are just a few questions I use when thinking through any communication. You're working with basic rhetoric principles, but people will judge you as a professional.

Even if you're not a "public speaking" person, it's crucial to be consistent in written communications. This communication could be in response to emails, or you can do written media interviews. Rather than doing a recorded phone interview (they're always recording, by the way), I'll ask them to email their questions for a response.

This asynchronous approach allows you to tighten your language and talking points, run it past your superintendent and district's communications lead, pass it around to a trusted board member, and then send it to the reporter. Should the need arise, you'll have copy-and-paste comments for constituent emails or other media inquiries.

Using written communication interviews is one of the best strategies for consistent outbound communications.

The language you use matters. Language is nuanced, and every word has a specific meaning. The neutrality example from earlier in this book demonstrates this principle perfectly.

The administration in one district used the term "intellectual freedom" to describe the agency provided to patrons. They wanted to allow everyone to discover what interested them, which is a great thing, but the board recognized that "intellectual freedom" was being misused to justify advocacy. They chose to reframe the value as "neutrality" instead.

Shifting away from intellectual freedom was a significant change for the board, as being a *neutral* district prevents the promotion of political candidates, parties, or ideologies. It was a move initially met with some minor resistance from staff members, but the community overall appreciated the decision and the direction to use "neutrality" across the district.

Not every stakeholder will understand your communications or why the board made specific language changes. That's okay. You're there to serve everyone, not please everyone. You have to make sure your communications and rhetoric are specific and intentional. I've seen it too many times where districts intend to say something beneficial, but because of their lack of messaging preparation, it backfires and causes more trouble than it solves.

Asking Questions

A key trait in principle-driven leaders is humility. Even in your elected role, there's room to learn and grow. You don't know everything, and acting as you do will make you look arrogant (not to mention ignorant). There's a difference between acting like you know everything and being confident. Confidence is okay, but pompous is not.

Asking questions, and a lot of them, is key to gaining understanding. Your superintendent and their leadership team are experts in their field. In most cases, they've spent a decade or more honing their craft and working through the educational landscape—partner with them to learn more and do your job better. When you succeed, they succeed—so don't get shy about asking questions.

Now, there are some considerations to remember as you start down the information-gathering part of your board journey. First, you'll want to plan a little bit. Do some background study on your own. Asking intelligent questions and following up for clarity shows you're committed to learning and partnership. Asking questions is one thing, but asking the right questions is even better.

Colorado, the state where I served, has an accreditation system that divides districts into five categories based on annual, state-level standardized testing. I've spent nearly ten years working with accreditation standards and processes at both charter and district levels. I finally realized I didn't know where the cut points came from to distinguish between any two categories, as these were non-standard and changed year to year.

I sat down with the Director of Curriculum and Instruction and asked her where the cut points came from. She didn't have an answer, so she asked a few of her staff members, who offered some insight but no definite answer. Since I didn't have the specifics I needed to understand the process, I went to a member of the State Board of Education, who took the question to the state's Department of Education. I finally got the clarity I needed from talking to state-level employees.

When I started asking questions about accreditation, I felt a little silly. With my experience in this process, I should have known *how* it worked by now, but I didn't. So,

I swallowed my pride and asked what I thought was a simple question. Little did I know that other experts from all levels across education didn't understand that part of the process either.

Education is complicated. There are too many minutiae for you to become an expert during your elected term, but asking questions will help inform your understanding and decision-making processes. It's not just okay to ask these questions, but your staff appreciates it. Asking questions and seeking advice prevents you from making decisions in a vacuum with implications you don't understand.

Strategic Questioning

Board meetings also provide opportunities to ask questions. I've used the dais to ask questions for two primary purposes: to help me understand and to help the community understand.

Helping me understand. As stated in the preceding paragraphs, I know I don't know everything. I always read my board packet ahead of time, and for the most part, everything made sense. Sometimes, however, something wouldn't click for me, either the outcomes, the data in a report, or the process. I would ask questions about all of those, as applicable, to ensure I understood where the district was heading and how it attained the data to make decisions. I also wanted to ensure the district adhered to its mission, vision, and board values in conducting its business.

Asking questions also held the district accountable. Since expectations require inspection, asking questions during our public meetings gave me a transparent way to hold the district accountable.

As I completed my board packet, I wrote down questions for the administration and sent them to the superintendent and the board president in advance. Part of our social contract was "no surprises." This norm set the expectation that no board member, superintendent, or cabinet member would try to fleece anyone during a public meeting. The board and administration are a team; teams don't intentionally make others look bad.

Sending these questions ahead of time accomplished two crucial things. First, it fulfilled my end of the social contract. It showed I was a team player and willing to follow our rules. It was a culture-setting move. The second thing it accomplished was allowing the administration time to prepare.

This preparation was part of why we had the "no surprise" clause in our social contract. Cabinet members knew the questions in advance and came prepared with answers. This preparation fostered deeper, more informed dialogue and enabled board members to ask meaningful follow-up questions for greater understanding. Partnering with the administration shows the board is a team player, seeking to understand rather than trying to play a "gotcha" game.

Helping the community understand. Another reason I asked questions was to help the community understand district methodologies and rationale. I can't tell you how many times I asked questions during a meeting that I already knew the answer to, but I wanted to make sure others in the community got the same answer and access to the information.

This tactic has helped disseminate information to the community to aid in understanding test scores and student outcomes, curriculum reviews, and accreditation status. As tough as it is for you, a board member, to walk into the ranks of education and weed through the jargon, it's even more so for the layperson in the community. Asking questions to help frame these concepts in a way your average stakeholder can grasp is vital to transparency in your district.

Other Key Strategies

I've also worked with the administration to prepare a line of questioning to help get a specific message and understanding into the public realm. I typically used this method to address community concerns. As the elected representative, you can show that you're listening to your constituents and community and allow the district to rebut or address those concerns directly.

Partnering with the district to ask specific questions is a tool I've shared with many districts. It can effectively bring understanding or a particular message to the public. I'd caution you against overusing it, but the right questions at the right times can be invaluable to you as a board member and to the district itself.

« »

The strategies listed above are tools for you to add to your toolbox as a school board member. Each of them has a purpose in implementing Values-Based Governance. They continue to push through the core tenets, increasing transparency and building trust, to set your district up for long-term success.

Homework – Chapter 12

1. Identify a current governing policy you disagree with. How could you use shared values to advocate for a change?

2. Draft three talking points on a contentious district issue that aligns with your board's values and mission.

3. Describe a situation where asking questions during a board meeting could help increase transparency for your community.

4. Outline a strategy to build a collaborative relationship with your superintendent while in the ideological minority.

5. Reflect on your most challenging board interaction. Which strategy from this chapter (leading from the minority, strategic communication, asking better questions, or building relationships) would have helped most? How will you apply it going forward?

Part IV:
The Resources

I've given you the model for Values-Based Governance and its implementation strategies throughout this book, but frameworks are only as good as your ability to put them into practice. Part IV provides the concrete tools you need to implement Values-Based Governance in your district successfully. You'll find a detailed 91-day implementation timeline to guide your initial rollout, assessment tools to evaluate your progress and build team alignment, and troubleshooting guidance for the challenges you're likely to encounter. These aren't theoretical concepts; they're practical resources, grounded in real-world experience, to help you navigate the complexities of organizational change. Whether you're just starting your VBG journey or working through implementation challenges, these tools will help ensure your efforts translate into meaningful improvements for students.

13
thirteen

Chapter 13:
Implementation Timeline

Chapter Summary:

In this chapter, you'll find a practical 91-day implementation timeline for Values-Based Governance. You'll see specific milestones for developing foundational documents, reviewing policies, and embedding VBG into your district's operations. This roadmap provides clear guideposts while allowing flexibility for your district's unique pace and circumstances.

Properly implementing Values-Based Governance (VBG) takes time—your district needs VBG to permeate the culture before you'll see the benefits. The timeline below provides guideposts for moving forward.

Every district moves at its own pace. You can progress quickly or slowly, and you can skip steps if they don't apply. For example, if your foundational documents already meet the criteria from Chapter 9, you can skip revisions.

Work with your administrative team to request information in advance. If your district faces an immediate crisis, see Chapter 16 for an accelerated 30-day implementation approach.

The 91-Day Plan

By Day 1: Tell People About Your New Efforts with VBG

Communication is a big key to the successful implementation of Values-Based Governance. You should start right out of the gate by telling your community that you've decided to undertake this effort and how it will benefit the students in your schools.

By Day 7: Mission, Vision, and UVP Review

The first part of your implementation will be to build your decision lens. Before building it out, evaluate what you have, so gather your mission, vision, and UVP. Take them one at a time and compare them to the descriptions in Chapter 9. Don't worry about revising these now, just take a look and review them. You'll need to ask some uncomfortable questions to evaluate how well these items truly reflect your district.

Start with your mission. Does it describe the goal you want to accomplish? Is it action-oriented? Is it short and clear? Is it written in a way that will allow your staff to rally around it? Is it focused on students?

Move to your vision and review it. Does it paint a picture of the way you want the world to be in the future? Can it be plastered on a wall? Will it attract the type of employees you want to bring into the fold?

Now look at your Unique Value Proposition, if you have one. If not, just move on to the next phase. If your district has a UVP, take a hard look at it. Is it something that's actually unique about your district, or is it just some fancy marketing? Could it describe a nearby district?

By Day 21: Revise Mission, Vision, and UVP as Needed

These three documents must work together, so you'll want to develop them together. You can review the criteria from Chapter 9 as needed. In addition to working with your fellow board members, I recommend seeking some counsel from your administration and community members. You get to make the decision, but there's no harm in getting feedback and using this exercise to engage members of your community.

By Day 28: Develop Board Values Statements

Developing these values is work your board needs to do together. There are many ways to accomplish this, but I've outlined a process in Chapter 14 entitled "Shared Values Statement Exercise." I recommend carving out 4 hours or so to work through this process. At the end, you'll want a single, unified statement listing the core values you share as board members. These shared values become your compass during tough times. You'll be able to hold each other accountable, as this shared value document will provide common ground for wading through the tough times.

Once you've developed the mission, vision, UVP, and shared values statement, you'll want to push that message out to your community. Start with district employees. You'll want to work with your communication team to develop fliers, social media images, t-shirts, or anything else you think will help your refreshed focus on students permeate your culture.

By Day 35: Review Latest Student Data

Your district can measure student outcomes in several ways. Request a presentation to your board on the most recent student data. Depending on when you engage with VBG, the data you're reviewing could be months old. Look for data breakdowns by grade level and cohort (3rd in 2024, 4th in 2025, 5th in 2026, etc.). Reviewing both views gives you a more complete picture.

Here's why cohort data matters: I've worked in districts where a particular grade level—say, 6th grade—showed the lowest performance in a given year. At first glance, you might think there's an issue with that grade level or perhaps the transition to middle school. But when you track the cohort data, the real story emerges: those same students were the lowest-performing group in 5th grade the previous year, and in 4th grade the year before. The problem wasn't the grade level—it was a specific cohort of students struggling as they moved through the system. This analysis allows you to invest more resources or reduce class size to help those students who need it most. These data trends will provide the information you need for the next step: setting goals for your superintendent.

By Day 42: Set Goals for Superintendent

You should have some goals already in place for your superintendent. Start by reviewing them against your mission, vision, and UVP that were developed by Day 21. You want to make sure the goals you're targeting will advance your district in the right direction. If the goals align with the documents you've developed, you're good to go. If not, this is the time to revise and make the change. Remember, leadership is doing the right thing, especially when it's hard. Changing the superintendent's goals mid-year can be uncomfortable, but it might be necessary if the original goals didn't align with the district's mission or focus on academic outcomes.

Note: If you're going to change the superintendent's goals mid-year, you *must* include them in that conversation.

By Day 49: Develop Your Superintendent Evaluation

The evaluation process is another exercise in alignment. You likely already have some tool you're using to evaluate your superintendent, but for this timeline, you want to ensure that it aligns with the goals you set in the last step. Make sure that the goals you've set are how you're evaluating the superintendent. Remember from Chapter 10 that you want to use the proper yardstick to measure outcomes and the right process to evaluate your superintendent. You must hold your superintendent accountable to the established goals.

Note: You can use the 4A Framework template from Chapter 10 (provided in full in Chapter 14 and at ChalkForge.com)

By Day 63: Update Governing Policies

The last piece needed for the Decision Lens to be complete is your policy book. Since the governing policies are where you input values, this is where you start. Remember from Chapter 7 that operational policy *must* align with governing policy. Take some time to review your governing policies and ensure they reflect your mission, vision, and shared values. Focus on tweaking existing policy language rather than rewriting the entire policy book. You might add a couple or remove a few, but this work should be more along the lines of minor changes rather than wholesale updates.

By Day 91: Operational Policy Review Underway

The administrative review will take quite a bit of time to complete. These policies are constantly in flux, based on state law, federal law, specific situations within your district, best practices, and governing policy. Having some patience with this review is advised, but don't allow your district to lose sight of the need to review and update these policies. Have your superintendent send weekly or bi-monthly reports listing policy updates with links to redline versions. These updates provide assurances to the board that the administrative team is carrying forward the VBG work.

« »

And voila!

That's your road map to implementing Values-Based Governance in 91 days. Remember that it'll take more time for these new foundational documents to seep into the culture. It would be good to test this when you're in school buildings and ask employees you see about the district's mission, vision, and unique value proposition. Now, don't approach this like trivia night; instead, engage staff members in conversations about these foundational documents and their use of Decision Lens.

The other significant piece of this is accountability, which doesn't happen overnight. Just because you put evaluations in place doesn't mean there has been accountability baked into each building and administrative level throughout your district.

Keep up the work, and you'll see the benefits from implementing VBG with each graduating class.

14
fourteen

Chapter 14:
Assessment and Planning Tools

Chapter Summary:

In this chapter, you'll find assessment and planning tools to support your VBG implementation. The *Self-Assessment* helps you evaluate your board's current effectiveness, the *Shared Values Exercise* guides you through building board unity, and the *User Story Template* ensures you understand real problems before creating policy solutions. These tools work together to help you develop a strong foundation and maintain momentum throughout your VBG journey.

Self-Assessment

Alignment and Focus:

- Can every board member recite the district's mission from memory?
- When did you last make a decision using the Decision Lens process?
- How often does the board communicate with the community?
- When you do communicate, what percentage aligns with your foundational documents and supports student achievement?

Behavioral Indicators:

- How many board members attended the last graduation ceremony?
- How many school events have board members attended in the past year?
- When did the board last change its mind based on student outcome data?
- How engaged is each board member during your meetings? Are members on their phones during the meeting?
- Do board members consistently follow the agreed-upon code of conduct and meeting norms?

Culture Check:

- Would your superintendent describe the board as supportive partners or obstacles?
- Do staff members approach board members with ideas, or avoid them?
- How does your community generally view the school board?

Assessments and Planning Tools

Data-Driven Evidence:
- What was the trend in student achievement in your district over the past three years?
- How many superintendents has your district had in the last five years?
- What percentage of board agenda items directly relate to academics?
- What has been your employee retention rate over the past three years?
- Are there trends from exit-interview data?

Shared Values Statement Exercise

Below is the process I've used when working with boards to develop a shared values statement. Feel free to modify as you see fit. I recommend doing this work off-site, away from your regular district work. Pulling your board away from the familiar allows you to reset and focus on the task at hand.

Set up the room with an easel in the corner and a few markers for note-taking. Set up a table with chairs around it so that everyone can see each other. Bring sticky notes and additional markers, so there are enough for each board member. Have printed copies of three different governing policies for each participant.

Step 1. Start by framing the conversation. Review the Shared Values section from Chapter 9 and discuss why this work is valuable to your district. These are shared values, which means you're trying to find where the board's values align/intersect. Just because something doesn't make it to the final cut doesn't mean it's not important, just that the board doesn't agree as a whole.

Step 2. Give everyone five sticky notes and a marker.

Step 3. Spend 20 minutes or so, allowing board members to reflect on their core values and write one on each sticky note. If anyone needs additional stickies, that's okay.

Step 4. Go around the room, with each board member reading one core value and placing it on a wall near the front.

Step 5. Group the stickies by theme/value as much as possible, eliminating outliers.

Note that this can be tricky because someone wrote these down for a reason. A moderator helps by neutralizing personal history and objectively narrowing the values list.

Assessments and Planning Tools

After Step 5 is also a good time to take a break if emotions are getting high.

Step 6. Work each themed value-set into short phrases/taglines.

Step 7. Create a single statement that ties the themed phrases into a cohesive structure.

Step 8. Review each policy on the printed sheets against the shared values statement to see how it works in practice. Check to see that the new shared values statement doesn't conflict with the district's mission or vision.

Step 9. Each board member signs their name to the statement, demonstrating support.

That's the exercise. Some boards will take more time than others to complete this work, but stick with it. If you need to have subsequent meetings to get through it, that's fine.

The important thing is that your board reaches an agreement on a statement they can use as a guiding light for policy and decisions. I recommend having the statement posted on the district's website. It's transparent and shows the board is doing work. It also makes this values statement accessible to employees through Decision Lens.

User Stories in Policy Development

I spent time in the tech industry, specifically in Agile software development. One of the core features of Agile is the *user story*. We used the template below whenever we considered new functionality. It takes the simple form of:

As a ___(who)___, I would like ___(what)___, because ___(why)___.

The first blank defines the role of the person making the request, the *who* of the function, if you will. The person here could be an end-user, an administrator, a developer, or any other role you can think of. The second blank is the actual function, or *what* the system needs to do, and the final blank is the rationale, or the *why* behind the function.

The user story focuses on how the system should operate, not how to do it. Sometimes, the person writing the user story would take a roundabout approach to something because they didn't understand how the software worked behind the scenes. Understanding the *why* behind the *what,* so the actual coders could best figure out the *how.*

The above is an excellent template for making policy in your district. For example, a parent could have approached a board member at the grocery store and said that the district doesn't communicate. The board member goes to the administration, and they start a weekly newsletter to provide parents with updates. Now, you, as the board member, call the concerned parent to explain how you helped close the communication gap. Unfortunately, the parent turns on you and says that you haven't fixed the issue. You go back to the administration and tell them the parent is still upset. That parent gets labeled as someone who "is never satisfied," and the district moves on, patting itself on the back.

How is everyone feeling right now? The district has worked to increase communication, but rather than solving issues, it has now driven a wedge between the district and

Assessments and Planning Tools

the parent who was bold enough to approach a board member with the problem. Do you think the parent will continue to raise issues in the future?

What if you had the parent complete the form above and submit it to the administration for review? It could look something like this:

> As a _parent of an elementary school student_, I would like _increased communication about upcoming activities_, because _I didn't know about my kid's recital and I missed it_.

Using this template really helps frame the problem, doesn't it? The district's newsletter never would have worked. The parent mentioned above missed a pivotal moment in their student's life. Can you feel the frustration? Armed with this information, the superintendent can talk to the building principal to find out what had happened that led to this. Maybe this needs to be a new policy, but perhaps it doesn't.

Perhaps the school sent paper fliers home in the student's backpack, but the student accidentally threw them in the trash can. The school tried to communicate, but it didn't reach the intended recipient. Utilizing this user story model can help narrow down policy to solve the correct problems for your community effectively.

Superintendent Evaluation

1. Academic Performance

Math:	Increase	Decrease	Stagnant
ELA:	Increase	Decrease	Stagnant

2. Attainment of Growth and Achievement Goals
    Top Priority Goals:
    -
    -
    -

Were all goals met?	Yes	No
If not, were they critical misses?	Yes	No

3. Adherence to Policy and Expectations

Were all policies followed?	Yes	No
Were all stated expectations met?	Yes	No

4. Associations with the Community

Students:	Good	Improve	Neutral
Parents:	Good	Improve	Neutral
Teachers:	Good	Improve	Neutral
Taxpayers:	Good	Improve	Neutral
Businesses:	Good	Improve	Neutral

Areas of strength: Areas for improvement:

Areas for follow-up/Action items:

15 fifteen

Chapter 15:
New Board Member Survival Kit

Chapter Summary:

In this chapter, new board members will find essential quick-reference information for their first months of service. You'll get reminders about role differentiation, meeting preparation strategies, key personnel to know, important terminology, and practical applications of VBG principles. This chapter serves as your go-to guide for quick answers or clarification.

There is a steep learning curve whenever you join a new organization as a board member. Even if you have years of experience serving on previous boards, you'll still need time to get up to speed. Each organization has its own values, culture, and customs. Each organization has different titles for the staff that you'll interact with, and even similar titles can have different roles and duties assigned to those titles.

With that in mind, this chapter contains a handful of tools and resources that can help you be effective in your new role faster. All of the items below are available as a single, free printable in the resources section at ChalkForge.com.

Role Differentiation Reminders

Board:

- Define "what" and "why"
- Set vision/mission
- Establish values
- Maintain accountability

Administration:

- Implement "how"
- Execute vision/mission
- Reflect values
- Create and enforce policy

Board Meeting Preparation

- Read Board Packet
- Send questions to the board chair/superintendent 48 hours in advance
- Research unfamiliar agenda items
- Ask for support ahead of time, if needed
- Review the district's mission, vision, and values statement
- Pack any notes/questions you have prepared
- Bring a notepad, pen, Robert's Rules, and other reference materials

Key Personnel

Superintendent: _____

Chief Finance Officer: _____

Curriculum Director: _____

Comms Director: _____

Attorney: _____

Board Chair: _____

Board Secretary: _____

Others: _____

_____

_____

_____

Key Terms and Definitions

IEP: *(Individualized Education Program)* Specialized plan for students receiving Special Education services

504: Accommodations for students with disabilities to access general education

IDEA: *(Individuals with Disabilities Education Act)* Grant from the Department of Ed to assist with SPED funding

Title I: Federal dollars for schools with high low-income populations

DAC/SAC: District/School Accountability Committee

MTSS: Multi-Tiered System of Supports

TOSA/TOA: Teacher on (Special) Assignment

PLC: Professional Learning Communities

NAEP: *(National Assessment of Educational Progress)* Congressionally mandated assessment of how students perform in various subjects across the country - district, state, and national results

Achievement: Student performance against grade-level standards

Growth: Improvement by a student in a single year

Values-Based Governance in Practice

Definition: *an approach to leading and stewarding an organization where decisions and actions are guided by core values, aligning personal, organizational, and stakeholder principles, aiming for ethical and effective management.*

Write your district's information below:
   Mission:

   Vision:

   Values:

Core Tenets of VBG:
- Strategic Alignment
- Policy Development
- Cultural Adaptation

Reminders
- Keep your focus on student success.
- Seek first to understand, not to show how smart you are.
- No surprises: we're all on the same team.
- When there's something you don't understand, pause and ask.
- Leadership is doing the right thing, especially when it's hard.

16
sixteen

Chapter 16:
Troubleshooting Guide

Chapter Summary:

In this chapter, you'll find solutions to common implementation challenges and resistance patterns. You'll learn how to address superintendent resistance, board member opposition, community pushback, and resource constraints. This troubleshooting guide helps you navigate obstacles and maintain momentum in your VBG implementation.

This chapter identifies some common areas where you or your board may encounter resistance when implementing Values-Based Governance. Each situation will be unique, but the general guidance below is for your district to use in navigating issues. Nothing in the following section will be revolutionary, but sometimes the practical aspects need reinforcement. We're not talking about shiny tools or buzzwords, but rather basic, simple strategies for dealing with opposition.

1. Other board members are actively fighting the framework.

Whoever on your board is championing the VBG efforts should sit down with each reluctant board member to ask why they're fighting the framework. Understanding when they started opposing the effort could be a key indicator. Something might have gone awry.

For instance, if they started fighting after the shared values statement, they could be frustrated that the final statement didn't accurately reflect one of their values. Or community members they trust didn't like the shared statement, and now they've adopted the group's values as their own and are actively undermining the district's work. In this case, remind them that the shared statement's purpose is to establish common ground for decision-making, while they can still maintain their personal values as part of their paradigm.

The rationale for their opposition will vary, which will impact how you respond. Generally, just keep pushing back to shared values, district mission/vision, and why they're on the board in the first place.

Asking them bluntly, "Do you think your current behavior is helping our students succeed?" might be a key question in helping bring them from active, open opposition to appeasement.

Troubleshooting Guide

2. What if our board members can't agree on shared values?

It should be a priority to reach a point where everyone can agree on some shared values. The more value themes you try to incorporate, the harder it will be to get everyone together. At the end of the day, you should all agree that students deserve the best education possible. Start there. Find some common ground, anything you can get everyone to agree on, and build from there.

I'm not at all saying this will be easy, but you should be able to find somewhere to start.

3. The superintendent is undermining VBG implementation.

If your superintendent is undermining the VBG implementation, it could be a symptom of a bigger issue. Where else could the superintendent be undermining the board? This act of subordination would call for a straightforward conversation between the board president and the superintendent. Something like, "This is the direction the board believes the district needs to go to serve the community. It might be uncomfortable, but our students can't afford for you and the administration to be working against the board. It's unprofessional behavior and sets a bad example for our students. Maybe it's time for you to think about whether this district is somewhere you can continue to see yourself working. Let's draft a mutual separation agreement, if needed, to make this amicable for all parties."

At the end of the day, VBG can't be successful if your superintendent is fighting your board and undermining the effort. They need to either get on board or you'll need to find someone who can support these efforts. You must implement VBG with fidelity, as the superintendent might be struggling with hypocrisy between the board's rhetoric and actions. Make sure you're doing your part before calling them to the mat.

4. Community groups are organizing against values-based policies.

Human nature is to resist change, as the status quo is the path of least resistance. Whenever you implement new frameworks or methodologies, you'll likely get community pushback about cost, time, or any other number of things. Some of these are valid, so actively listen to what the community is saying.

It could be cost-related, stating the district could pay teachers more, or it could provide more para support if they weren't implementing VBG. The cost to implement this is relatively low and probably won't affect the overall staffing budget.

Another potential root of the community's opposition is that they don't understand what VBG is or how it will affect their students. They see it as another fad that isn't significantly different and will take staff time and attention away from students. Although possible, it's unlikely that the time taken away will impact students much. Most of the work is being done at the district and administrator level, leaving teachers and other staff to continue their positive interactions with students. A potential approach is to hold an open forum to discuss VBG myths and provide details on your implementation timeline and process.

5. Staff are saying this is just another fad that will pass.

Staff considering this another fad is a likely scenario, especially if your district has made other changes recently. It would provide fuel to the fire, giving them something to point at and say, "We were just doing this, now we're doing that. Next month it'll be something different again." Unfortunately, this is too common an occurrence in education.

In many cases, this type of sentiment is a defense mechanism in which leadership is getting pushback from their staff, and these administrators' actions are "protecting" their staff from the district by playing a blocking role. The pushback could stem from perceived additional work that staff can't take on, or from misinformation about the framework and what it will do. Staff might think it will require them to go against their own values to support the board's values. As you should know by now, that's not the case at all.

One way to help them see the stickiness of VBG is to hold an open forum for district and building leadership before fully diving into implementation. Ask them questions about concerns. One key feature is that this isn't a classroom technique. It doesn't add anything to teachers' plates, as other frameworks might. If anything, this is a tool to empower teachers and staff to make decisions that align with the district's foundational documents.

Once staff see that this empowers them rather than burdens them, you should see the oppositional rhetoric start to fade.

6. Staff/Administration is accusing our board of overreaching.

First, be sure you're not overreaching before you respond. There's a strong likelihood that your board is overreaching to ensure district policy and operations align with the foundational documents. Such overreach wouldn't be intentional; it would be a natural byproduct of monitoring the district's implementation of VBG.

Once you can rule out that you are overstepping, find out why they're saying this. Who's saying it? Is there a specific instance? Staff might feel uncomfortable about the way the board is redefining success or reorienting the district through the mission and vision.

The foundational documents and governing policies all fall under the board's purview. Setting superintendent goals and truing up the evaluation process are board-overseen items, and shouldn't be causing problems. The only place you might get into trouble with overreach during your VBG implementation is if you cross the line between governing and operational policies.

If your board (or members of your board) are guilty of micromanagement and overstepping the board's role, then back up. If not, keep carrying on.

7. The implementation of VBG has stalled.

Having a defined implementation timeline and appointing a "VBG Champion" will help keep the process moving forward. Because the board controls the process up to the operational policy reviews, one of the most susceptible areas for stalling is the review and update of operational policy. District offices are busy, and then get busier. It's easy for IEP compliance issues and student safety concerns to take priority over policy updates.

Prioritization of urgent matters is why I recommend having regular updates to the board on the progress of the operational policy updates. It will hold the superintendent accountable for steady progress, even if it's in small increments.

You could even appoint a board member to sit on the committee that's reviewing the policies. Even if the board member serves in an ex officio capacity, their presence will help maintain integrity throughout this process. The committee could ask questions about the policy's intent. The board member then knows and can report back to the board regarding the district's progress in policy development.

If the process has stalled for other reasons, it would be beneficial to call a meeting to discuss it. Call it a "VBG Reset" meeting, where you talk through the implementation timeline, completed items, and the next steps the district should take to build momentum again.

Troubleshooting Guide

8. Our district is experiencing leadership changes. How do we keep momentum?

When bringing on a new leader, one of the biggest concerns is that they're value-aligned with the direction the board is going. Make sure your mission, vision, UVP, and value statements are up front and clearly stated in any posting you make. Bring it up again during interviews and in every conversation you have with candidates and newly appointed leaders. Constantly keeping these foundational documents in front of your leadership team will a) show them the board is resolute, b) lead by example, since it's in all of your communication, the administration should reflect the foundational documents in theirs, and c) give the new leader no excuse to deny knowing where you're going.

The above ensures the new leader is knowledgeable and willing to execute the board's mission and vision, but maintaining momentum requires the board to know where the implementation stands. Make sure the timeline is available, that any completed items are marked off, and that there is a plan from the previous leader (or from assistants) outlining the next steps, so the new leader has time to acclimate while still executing on the remaining implementation needs.

9. Our district is in crisis mode. How do we implement VBG quickly?

If your district is in crisis, you have to focus on achieving stability as quickly as possible. You must navigate the change process carefully. To manage this appropriately, you've got to communicate regularly with your community. You're also going to modify the actual implementation steps and skip some to try to reach a state of equilibrium for your district.

You should send weekly updates to your community as your board begins implementing Values-Based Governance. This proactive communication is one of the best ways to start building back trust and moving your district out of the crisis.

Consider bringing in an outside moderator to help navigate this process when your district is in crisis mode.

By Day 1: Tell People About Your New Efforts with VBG

Communication is a big key to the successful implementation of Values-Based Governance. You should start right out of the gate by telling your community that you've decided to undertake this effort and how it will benefit the students in your schools. Especially in crises, you need increased communication.

By Day 7: Revise Mission, Vision, and UVP as Needed

You need to get these foundational documents together quickly, so you can use them as a base for communication and messaging.

By Day 14: Set Shared Values Statements

Focus on quality over quantity. You can revisit your values statement later, but you need to demonstrate that your board can come together and reach an agreement. Demonstrating unity to your community is critical during a crisis.

By Day 21: Goal Setting for the Superintendent

The board should focus the superintendent's goals on short-term results that will start moving the district out of the turmoil and into calmer waters.

By Day 30: Governing Policy Review

During this review, focus on getting the policies aligned with your foundational documents. You want to get them aligned, but you don't need to make wholesale changes. Finalizing governing policy is another area where you can take a second pass once the district has had time to stabilize.

Troubleshooting Guide

The ongoing operational policy review is less important when trying to stabilize. There will be time to review and revise the shared values statement, the governing policy, and subsequent operational policies once your district is out of crisis mode. Remember, the focus is on getting your district to stabilize at this point.

If you have questions about any of the steps mentioned above, more detailed descriptions of each step can be found in Chapter 13.

Conclusion

The Choice Before You

You've reached the end of this book, but you're standing at the beginning of something much more important: the opportunity to transform how your school board serves students.

Everything you've read (the framework, the strategies, the stories of success and failure) comes down to a simple choice. Will you be a board member who makes excuses, or one who makes a difference?

What We've Covered

Through these pages, we've built a comprehensive framework for effective school board governance:

In Part I, we established the foundation. You learned that good governance requires accountability, leadership, and teamwork. You discovered how different types of values (personal, board, district, societal, and group) interact and sometimes conflict. You understood the unique challenges facing school boards, from dealing with involuntary families to addressing organizational drift.

In Part II, we constructed the Values-Based Governance model. The three core tenets work together to create sustainable change:

- Strategic Alignment defines who you are as an organization through mission, vision, values, and unique value proposition (UVP)
- Policy Development embeds those values into the organization's DNA
- Cultural Adaptation implements those values in daily practice throughout the district

In Part III, we provided practical implementation strategies. You learned how to build foundational documents that guide decision-making. You discovered the critical importance of accountability, not just holding others accountable, but modeling it yourself. You also saw how to make changes that outlast your individual term on the board.

In Part IV, we provided practical resources to help you with implementing Values-Based Governance in your district. These resources included a 91-day timeline, assessment and evaluation support, a survival kit, and a troubleshooting guide to help you move the effort forward and make a difference for your students and your community.

The Power of the Framework

Values-Based Governance isn't just another management theory. It's a proven approach that transforms how boards operate and, more importantly, how effectively they serve students. When you implement VBG, several things happen:

Clarity emerges. Decisions become easier because you have a clear framework for evaluation. The Decision Lens helps everyone in the organization make choices that align with your mission and values.

Conflicts diminish. When board members operate from shared values focused on student outcomes, personal agendas fade into the background. You'll still have disagreements, but they'll be productive debates about the best way to serve kids, not political battles.

Culture shifts. As you model values-based decision-making in the boardroom, it ripples throughout the organization. Teachers, principals, and support staff begin making decisions through the same lens.

Results improve. Most importantly, student outcomes get better. When everything in your district aligns around academic success, kids benefit. Test scores rise, graduation rates improve, and college and career readiness increase.

The Reality of Implementation

Let me be honest with you: implementing Values-Based Governance isn't easy. You'll face resistance. Some will question your motives. Others will prefer the path of least resistance, the status quo, because it's comfortable, even if it's ineffective.

Remember my opening line about being "booed, cheered, and haggled by Satanists and religious zealots"? That's not hyperbole. When you commit to doing the right thing for students, some people won't like it. They'll attack your character, question your qualifications, and try to make serving on the school board as unpleasant as possible.

But here's what I've learned: the temporary discomfort of implementing change is nothing compared to the lasting regret of knowing you could have made a difference and chose not to.

Your Legacy

Every decision you make as a board member affects students. Some of those students are sitting in classrooms right now, struggling with reading or math, wondering if anyone cares about their success. Others are elementary students who won't graduate for another decade, but your decisions today will shape their educational experience. What legacy do you want to leave?

Do you want to be remembered as someone who got bogged down in political fights while students struggled? Someone who focused on adult concerns instead of academic outcomes? Someone who maintained the status quo because change was hard?

Or do you want to be remembered as someone who transformed your district? Someone who dared to align everything around student success? Someone who proved that school boards can be forces for positive change in their communities?

Here's something that might surprise you: the impact of Values-Based Governance extends far beyond your district boundaries.

When you model effective governance, other boards take notice. When your district's academic outcomes improve, neighboring communities ask questions. When your culture of accountability and focus spreads, it can influence state-level education policy.

I've had board members share stories of transformed relationships with superintendents, improved staff morale, and (most importantly) better outcomes for kids.

You're not just changing your district. You're contributing to a movement that could transform public education.

The Students Are Waiting

As I write this conclusion, millions of students are getting ready for another school day. They're packing backpacks, eating breakfast, and heading to schools governed by local boards of education.

Some of those students will attend districts led by boards that practice Values-Based Governance. These kids will benefit from clear mission-driven policies, accountability systems that ensure they're learning, and cultures that prioritize their success above all else.

Other students will attend districts led by dysfunctional boards that prioritize politics over pedagogy, avoid accountability, and allow mission drift to consume resources intended for learning.

Which type of district do you want to lead?

Your Next Steps

If you're ready to implement Values-Based Governance in your district, start with the fundamentals:

1. Complete the homework assignments from each chapter. These aren't busy work; I've designed these questions to help you internalize and apply the concepts.
2. Utilize the 91-Day Implementation Guide from Chapter 13, which will step you through the process to implement VBG in your district. Adapt it to your district and work to make constant progress.
3. Assess your current foundational documents. How well does your mission, vision, and values statement align with student outcomes? Use the criteria from Chapter 9 to evaluate them.
4. Build relationships with your superintendent and fellow board members. Change is easier when you're working together rather than fighting each other. You don't have to be friends, but you must be professional.
5. Start with yourself. Model the behavior you want to see throughout the district. Use the Decision Lens for your own choices. Focus your questions and comments on student outcomes.

6. Be patient but persistent. Cultural change takes time, but it's worth the wait. Stay focused on your mission even when others get distracted.

A Personal Note

When I first joined a school board, I had no idea what I was getting into. I made mistakes, learned hard lessons, and sometimes wondered if the effort was worth it.

Then I attended my first graduation ceremony. Watching those kids walk across the stage, some of them the first in their families to graduate, reminded me why this work matters. Every policy decision, every budget discussion, every difficult conversation was worth it for that moment.

That's what Values-Based Governance is really about: creating more of those moments. More students are succeeding. More families are celebrating. More communities are thriving because their schools are excellent.

The Call to Leadership

Our founders built this country on the principle of citizen leadership: ordinary people stepping up to serve their communities. School board service is one of the purest expressions of that principle.

But service isn't enough. We need effective service. We need leadership that makes a difference. Values-Based Governance gives you the tools to be that kind of leader. The framework is simple. The strategies work. The only question is whether you'll have the courage to implement them.

The students in your district deserve board members who prioritize their academic success. The community that elected you deserves leaders who can govern effectively. The profession of education deserves advocates who understand that excellence isn't optional. You have the opportunity to be all of these things.

Conclusion: The Choice Before You

*Leadership Is Doing the Right Thing,
Especially When It's Hard*

I've repeated this phrase throughout the book because it captures the essence of Values-Based Governance. It's not about doing what's easy or popular. It's about doing what's right for students, even when (or especially when) it's difficult.

The choice is yours. You can be a board member who goes along to get along, who avoids conflict, who settles for mediocrity. Or you can be a leader who transforms your district through Values-Based Governance.

I know which choice I hope you'll make. The students are counting on you. Don't let them down.

Final Homework Assignment

Before you close this book, complete this final reflection:

1. What is the most important thing you learned from this book?
2. What is one specific change you will make in how you approach your role as a board member?
3. How will you know if you're successfully implementing Values-Based Governance in your district?
4. What legacy do you want to leave as a school board member?

Write your answers down. Keep them visible. Review them regularly.

The students in your district deserve nothing less than your absolute best. Values-Based Governance will help you deliver it.

Now go. It's your turn to govern differently.

About the Author

Aaron Salt has served for over a decade on public boards in Colorado, including as founding board member and chair of a charter school, elected member and board president of a public school district, and appointed trustee and president of a public library district.

Salt's professional background spans business consulting, software development, and educational operations. He holds a Master's degree in Social Work from Florida State University and a Bachelor's degree in Psychology from Auburn University.

The Values-Based Governance framework presented in this book emerged from his experience leading organizations through challenging times. His governance philosophy centers on a principle he coined: "Leadership is doing the right thing, especially when it's hard."

Salt lives in Colorado with his wife and four children.

Acknowledgments

First and foremost, I want to thank Jesus Christ for giving me the courage and capacity to serve my community and take on the task of writing a book. Next (and also foremost), my beautiful bride and love of my life, Cortney. You have read through this manuscript several times and listened to me obsess over extremely minor details for months, and helped me fine tune so much of this manuscript. Not to mention how much you had to solo-parent during my time on the school boards. I can never thank you enough for your support over the past decade. You're my rock and dearest friend. To my kids, thank you for being you. You're the whole reason I started down this path. You are all fun, amazing kids with such a bright future. Thank you for your patience and still loving me when I snapped at you to "go back to bed" at 5:45am when I was neck deep in edits.

Next to a friend of mine, who I said I'd name in the acknowledgments if she gave me feedback on an early draft. You didn't follow through, so this is all you get. To Pastor Steve, thank your for your covering and unwavering support. I appreciate the cigars and fireside chats discussing leadership. Rick, I wouldn't have started this crazy ride without you, and I'm not sure I've forgiven you yet. Maybe 1 more lunch and we'll call it even. Brad and Jordan, I appreciate you taking time from your busy lives to give this a read through and provide thoughtful feedback on it. Your support has been encouraging through the process. Lauren, you've been a confidant, sounding board, and a missional anchor when things get rocky.

And finally, to all those I served with, both colleagues and administration/staff. I've had the privilege of working with some of the most capable, smart, and effective people. You've made my time on these boards a pleasure. I wouldn't change a minute of it. You guys are all rock stars.

www.ingramcontent.com/pod-product-compliance
Lightning Source LLC
Chambersburg PA
CBHW020535030426
42337CB00013B/862